FAMILY CIRCLE HOME DECORATING GUIDE

EDITORS:

CAROLYN BISHOP
FAMILY CIRCLE HOME FURNISHINGS/
EQUIPMENT EDITOR

DELPHENE RICHARDS
FAMILY CIRCLE INTERIOR
DESIGN EDITOR

ART DIRECTOR:
WILLIAM E. SCHULEIN

ASSOCIATE EDITOR:
JOANN FRANCIS GRAY

ASSISTANT ART DIRECTOR:
MARSHA CAMERA

COPY ASSOCIATE:
CONNIE GODDARD

ILLUSTRATIONS BY ONI

A New York Times Company Publication NYT

CONTENTS

Published simultaneously in U.S.A. and Canada by The Family Circle, Inc.,
a subsidiary of The New York Times Media Company, Inc.
Copyright © 1973 by The Family Circle, Inc. All rights reserved.
Title FAMILY CIRCLE registered U.S. Patent Office, Canada, Great Britain,
Australia and other countries. Marca registrada.
Printed in U.S.A. LC 73-11786. ISBN 0-405-09843-X.

Dear Home Decorator:

Furnishing a home is a necessity, often limited by space and budget. But decorating a home is a privilege, limited only by imagination and self-confidence. Everyone has the creative instinct to improve an environment, whether by changing a color or adding a flower. All that's needed is trust in one's instincts.

Instead of what is passing-faddish or super-costly, indulge yourself in your own experience and taste. Half the fun and satisfaction of decorating is being able to brazen it out for yourself with more ingenuity than income. Even the wealthiest people like to do a few things for themselves, such as making instead of buying, inventing rather than imitating, and restoring rather than discarding worn-out favorites. Add to imagination the simplest tools—hammer and nails, glue and staple gun, needle and thread, paint and brush—and it's possible to slipcover chairs, frame art, make cushions, refinish cabinets, paint door moldings, line china cabinets, appliqué window shades, fake ceiling beams. Add to imagination the simplest sources—auctions, thrift shops, five-and-dimes, family attics—and it's possible to find furnishings of grace and utility that are low in cost, high in pride.

So plunge right in. On the pages that follow you'll find information and guidance for every decorating situation you're likely to encounter, plus hundreds of dreamy ideas...not the fixed dreams that display rooms are made of, but rather dreams that you can fix yourself, in leisure time and in your own place, utilizing the resources of your past and present.

The Editors

DESIGN: PAT PLAXICO. AID. PHOTOGRAPHY: MALCOLM COOK.

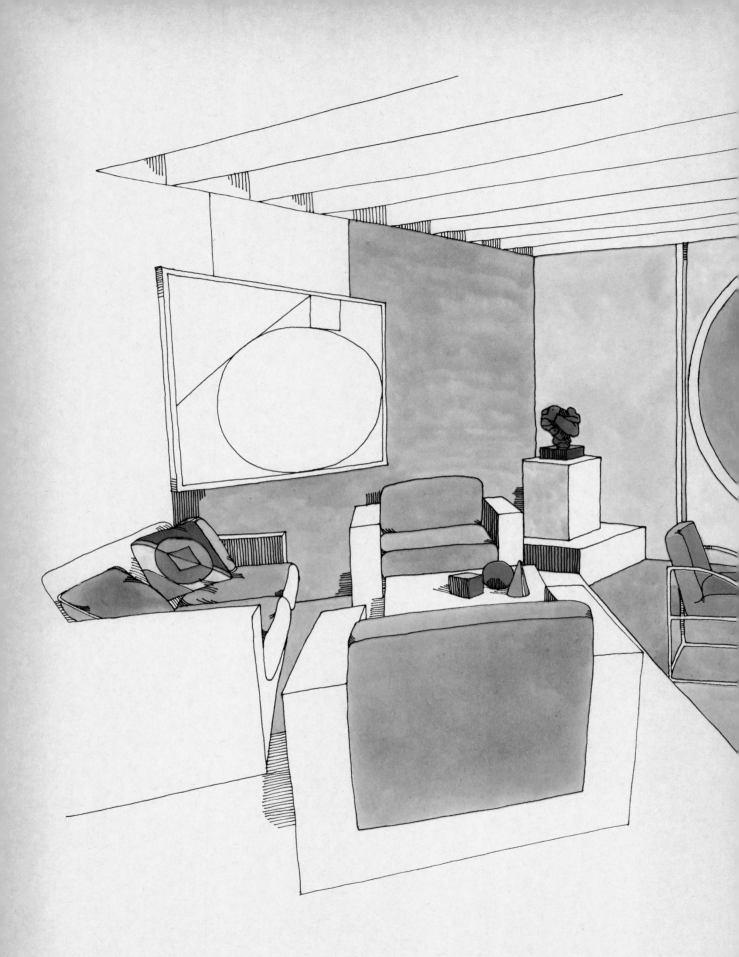

CHAPTER ONE

COLOR AND YOU

All colors are good, and you are entitled to choose favorites and indulge in them. Suit your gregarious self with yellow, soothe your passionate personality with purple, surrender your explosive side to red, edit nature for the best of its greens.

A brave new whorl of color frees decorating from past clichés of urban dirt-white and suburban safe-beige.

Mix, match, contrast, experiment. Adventure into off-beat pastels or bold poster primaries. Dare combinations in small doses that you couldn't be bribed to try on a large scale. Startle neutral schemes with brights. Heighten black's impact with stabs of hot pink, lime or lemon yellow. Run the range of reds from cold to hot, of blues from warm to cool.

Stay with a favorite hue forever, merely varying its values. Or, change frequently on whim—with a fresh coat of paint, a new slip-cover or curtains, an exchange of art from room to room, or simply by adding something as innocent as fresh flowers.

A study of color will have you talking like an expert. But only personal and spontaneous experimentation with color will have you decorating like one. To fully enjoy color be true to your own likes and dislikes.

If clashing colors stimulate you, clash them. If they jar you, try using complementary (opposites on the color wheel), analogous (neighboring colors) or mono-chromatic (tints and shades of a single color) schemes instead.

Color is entirely subjective and influenced by personal idiosyncrasies. If smoky blue reminds you of a sensual saxophone solo, and you want to feel sensual, use it. If puce (brownish purple) reminds you of elephant's breath and you abhor elephants, avoid it, even if it does go well with the rest of your color scheme.

Color expert Faber Birren reminds us that the way a person reacts to a color is significant and should be acknowledged when choosing colors for a home. Of course, there is a veritable googol (the numeral one, followed by 100 zeros) of colors in terms of hues, chromas, values, luminosity, shades and tints. Hue is any normal color

DESIGN: ONI. PHOTOGRAPHY: GEORGE NORDHAUSEN

such as green, blue, red, yellow. Chroma is the strength or intensity of that color. Value, its lightness or darkness. Luminosity refers to how it is affected by light. Tint and shade, to its range from pale to dark. In addition, it's also important to consider how one color affects another. Red makes yellow look greenish, for example—pleasant in a wallpaper or fabric design, but hardly suitable for a sallow-complexioned person to wear. This is nothing an amateur hasn't discovered for herself through clothes fashion and the use of cosmetics.

But beyond complexions are emotions and personality traits that are of far more interest to a home decorator. The colors you choose not only should reflect your personality, but do— if you want them to or not.

For instance, a preference for red signifies a positive personality; firey red, impulsive and vigorous; maroon, likable and generous. A preference for blue suggests the sensitive and secure; for blue-green, someone stable and detached; blue-red, temperamental, yet undemanding. Green is honest and loyal; turquoise, confident and sophisticated; yellow-green, intellectual and liberal. Within your color preferences it's your prerogative to play with the primaries (blue, yellow, red), to contrast them or use instead their secondary greens, oranges, purples, or to decorate mono-chromatically with varying tints and shades of a single color.

A color wheel—instant reference to the relationships of color, one to another—is pictured here to help you get started.

A Renoir-inspired wallpaper themes this cheerful hobby-bedroom and establishes its multicolored scheme. Notice the colors repeated throughout the room in nearly the same proportions—a foolproof formula to follow. As in the wildflowers of the paper, lemon yellow and lime green predominate. Apricot and pink are picked up in the gingham dress fabric used for dust ruffle, toss pillows and to edge the curtains.

DESIGN: JOHN WEBER, AID. PHOTOGRAPHY: VINCENT LISANTI

THE EASY, MEMORABLE MONOCHROMATIC SCHEME

Experts suggest that the most successful color schemes are the ones with the fewest colors. Certainly they are among the least demanding visually, and also among the simplest to plan. But, unless textures and patterns are varied, they can border on the monotonous. Monochromatic schemes—those using varying intensities from pale to bold, light to dark, of a single dominant color—are also among the most memorable.

Think of some of the rooms that have made lasting impressions on you. The White House, for example, is famous for its Gold Room, Green Room, Blue Room and brilliant Red Room. Their impact, however, depends somewhat on cooperation from the people within them. Knowing visitors will dress for the memorable room, rather than in competition with it. A Manhattan fashion editor, for example, recently recommended low-key, solid-color fashions for the Red Room, as opposed to a stylish Pucci dress that would compete for attention. This same fashion principle applies to decorating. To avoid monotony, fabrics and materials in a monochromatic room should be interestingly textured and varied, although not excessively.

Proper balance of texture and pattern is clear in this bedroom (opposite) featuring blue shag carpeting wall-to-wall, blue-and-white tablecloth-checked bedspreads, a blue-and-white porcelain lamp with navy pleated shade. Walls and wicker furniture are white deliberately, to show off the different blues to their best advantage. This cool and uncomplicated scheme, plus the simplicity of furnishings and the absolute absence of clutter, is an effective way to make a small room seem visually larger.

Yellow rooms, like the sun, can almost be too bright to stare at steadily. But there are ways of lidding the gaze (below left) with woods, small doses of contrasting colors and interesting patterns. Yellow is a favorite of idealists. The complementary pinks, oranges and greens used with it here in curtains, bedspread (foreground) and window shade trim, are favorite colors of warm, good-natured and loyal individuals. The resulting bed-sitting room has all these characteristics.

Window shades are of the room-darkening variety to prevent daylight from disturbing the late sleeping guest.

Green, especially sprout green (below right), is cool, fresh and rejuvenating in combination with lots of white—a perfect choice for a family breakfast nook. Mixed cane- and bamboo-patterned ceramic tile adds a crisp, clean look to the cool. Notice the use of molding to create architectural detailing—chair rail and wall panel—and to accentuate the combination of patterns. Under all is a totally white ceramic tile floor that wipes clean with a damp cloth, never mars or scuffs. Decorative additions include painted shutters, an old-fashion ceiling fan and plants. Nature's scheme is so basic you can change its mood by varying the tableware.

DESIGN: JULIE DENISON AND RAY KINDELL, AID

ADVANCING ORANGES RECEDING BLUES

Reds, oranges and yellows create a warm and cheerful atmosphere anywhere—and are especially welcome in a room with a feeble, diffused, northern exposure. Like the luminous glow of sunlight, reds, oranges and yellows are warm and advancing and literally seem nearer to the eye than blues and greens. An advancing scheme begins with color dominating the walls, ceiling or floor.

Like folk tunes orchestrated in the head, this orange room reaches out toward light and sound and people. You can expect companionship here, plus alert listening. Comfortable sofas conspire to good conversation. And a wall of art, music, books and games keeps attention focused on the egregious mix who meet here.

Pale blues and greens help to create a cool and restful atmosphere—and particularly in a room with a strong and sunny southern exposure. The diminutive patterns appear cooler than bigger, bolder ones. Textures, too, have cool when they combine smooth and touchable, as in smooth walls and touchable quilted bed throws.

Vinyl—especially blue-white-green "tiled" vinyl—used not only for flooring, but on bed posts and up wall in place of headboards, is also cooling and relaxing on sight and touch.

Windows are shuttered in white against relentless direct daylight. But, for the gray and rainy days and all-shadowy nights, one or two hot-colored velvet pillows store warmth.

This bedroom is literally swathed in no-wax flooring with a hand-painted tile look—seamless and flexible enough to wrap around posts, up walls, and across window seats.

DESIGN: VIRGINIA FRANKEL →

DESIGN: BIC JONSON, NSID. PHOTOGRAPHY: VAN DERVEER

THE BIG THEATRICAL FAMILY OF REDS

Red is one of decorating's most emotional colors, both to work with and live with. People see red when they're angry. Red means stop on warning signs. Red is the color of the hair of history's villains and clowns. Yet, certain shades of red are sacred (poppy), or heroic (scarlet), or divine (blood). Some people love red, but unlove its analogous oranges and mauves.

One thing about red is that there are no in-between reactions to it, like the shrugs that sometimes greet the color family of gray. Red is an attention getter in its faintest or most brazen hues, in accent or barnsize doses.

Witness its tint (pink) and analogous mauve-purple: an old bathroom (left) of only nostalgic value until transformed by painting the tub, covering walls and ceiling in a sweet-pink, shell-patterned vinyl and adding nappy new towels.

A big commitment to red in a suburban split-level (left) makes the loft sitting area a warm, inviting place to be. The same area in blue might have been translated as aloof.

Reds at their theatrical best, right, range from the cool of claret in crystal goblets, to a swath of warm plum in the carpeting, to a gradual ripening from orange to crimson in drapery panels. The result is a posh and polished room that expresses its owner's favorite pastime: entertaining there.

PHOTOGRAPHY: MARTIN HELFER. DESIGN: NANJA WILLIAMS.
LOCATION: LARWIN'S GREENBROOK, CORAM, L. I., N.Y.

THE NEUTRAL COLOR SCHEME:
A COLLABORATION WITH NATURE

Undemanding rooms are made of neutral, or no-color, schemes that rely on textures and nature and the people in them for impact. They are stages set for quiet communing. It's oddly impossible to be bored. You want to touch the materials, sniff the fragrances, feast on all shapes, respect or shatter the implicit silence of neutral, or no-color, rooms.

Unlike dynamic, colorful opposites, monochromes, primaries and multi-colors, neutral schemes do not demand comment, or that you buy balloons to go with them, or that you avoid Pucci fashions, or be in the least gregarious. Neutrals are counter-colors: non-blues and non-greens, mist-kissed, sun-baked, Grand Canyon sweet and organic as cornmeal, prune, celery, wheat, alfalfa, sunflower seed and soy, and perhaps a rush of gold. You can rest from exhaustion in a neutral-colored room. Or sit in yielding suede-looking director's chairs, surrounded by living greens (below). The wall here is a series of hinged louvered doors, neither polished nor painted, just left in a natural state. Colors are added or subtracted on whim, in table linens, fresh flowers and accessories.

A no-color kitchen (opposite), suddenly startled by the simple red of apples, is entirely of good wood looks, as natural as the elm trees from which its paneling derives.

A small, formal living room in a southwestern home (below) borrows its Indian neutrals from the sun-baked, New Mexico countryside.

The pale sand color of the love seats, accented with bark-colored welting, is repeated in the draperies—all very flattering to tactile stucco walls.

DESIGN: RUDOLPH SALAZAR, NSID. PHOTOGRAPHY: VINCENT LISANTI
LOCATION: RIO RANCHO, ALBUQUERQUE, NEW MEXICO

DARINGLY DIFFERENT: THE TWO-COLOR SCHEME

Inspirations for color schemes can originate with the furniture, with a personal color preference, with the demands of the room itself. A clever balance of two colors can help set off cherished designs, establish a mood, enlarge or diminish space, and add totally new interpretations.

In the room below, furniture inspires the color scheme. Wood-loving emerald green and discovered gold are used in instinctive natural balance to set off the beauty of polished oak designs. More green is used in carpeting, painted inside shutter treatment and valance; for a toss pillow, to line bookshelves and as mats for shadowbox art. Less gold is used in the plush velvet sofa and smooth, woven-textured wing chair. To help

DESIGN: GILBERT A. GRAY, AID.
PHOTOGRAPHY: EARL McINTOSH

square off an otherwise angular room, one wall has been pulled in by painting it charcoal, the other wall has been extended by covering it in a charcoal-and-white laminated fabric.

Personal color preference dictates the room below. Purple is unusual and exclusive, often the choice of artists. Overdoses suggest self-indulgence. Brazen values of purple shout of passionate rebellion. Balanced combinations of purple with a second color, such as white, however, show sensitivity. White helps discipline purple's temperament; helps subtract the "ot'' from "zealot," leaving only an aura of "zeal" for living.

On the other hand, a room can determine the color combination. A clinical, tile-white modern bath, lighted by ghostly fluorescents, was transformed by black-and-beige newsprinted vinyl covering for walls, ceiling, and lavanette, and by plain linen-like vinyl for the dado, or lower wall. Black painted two-by-fours add both architectural interest and bonus shelf space. Modern lucite ceiling light replaces the old bowl type.

CONCEPT: BIC JONSON, NSID. STYLING: GILBERT A. GRAY, AID. PHOTOGRAPHY: VAN DERVEER

DESIGN: ELROY EDSON, AID. PHOTOGRAPHY: VINCENT LISANTI

The one-room Manhattan apartment of a gregarious young woman leads the life of a three- or more-room apartment through a choice of colors that (1) reflect personal interests (2) help divide up space without compacting it. Instead of room dividers or partitions that separate eating from sleeping from contemplation, color does the job in terms of amounts used, how it is used, and what textures are involved.

The welcoming entry is decorated in a sociable "femcee" orange, from the orange of the carpeting to orange vinyl-upholstered wall and orange velvet dining chairs. Yellow begins at the threshold of a neat and contemporary living area and is continued through seating, ceiling and wall vinyl, and a second, living area carpet. An "L" or alcove of green vinyl supplies a more private and introspective place apart.

Color expert Faber Birren says "The social traits of those who like green are quite similar to the traits of those who like orange." The subtle difference is that "orange is a city color, green is a suburban." Within this small L-shaped space exists both city and suburb.

Living is assigned to the largest corner of the apartment, a combination of music, reading, conversation, entertaining and sleeping, supplied by a judicious choice of furniture that includes a deceptively sofa-looking queen-size sleeper. All pet colors combine to tell the story of both open hospitality and guarded privacy. Viewless windows in clumsy assymetrical spacing are decorated with alternating panels of wide and narrow window shades that are done by laminating fabric to shade cloth using an iron-on method.

CHAPTER TWO

DECORATING STYLES

Styles in decorating span continents, cultures and centuries—from the authority of 15th century Spanish to the exuberance of Italian Renaissance, from the unparalleled grace of Louis XV to the elite of American Traditional to the modern of Bauhaus.

In recent years we've witnessed the emergence of still a new trend—a free and artful blending of countries, cultures and centuries into a style that's come to be known as eclectic—in a term, a suit-your-own-self or "new American" kind of decorating.

Your own good taste dictates the style or combination of styles that's best for you —be it predominantly Early American, comfortable contemporary or ornamental Spanish or Mediterranean.

GUIDELINES TO STYLES: EMOTIONAL AND INNOVATIVE

You may yearn for a grandeur that is past, or feel nostalgia for an era long gone, sympathize with the pioneers or fantasize about European courts, seek an identity that is secure in history or prefer to create a fresh new history, unhaunted by ago. Today it's impossible to imitate, even improve upon, all of the world's decorating styles. Mass manufacture helps to reproduce masterpieces in furniture, faithful in every detail to their classic prototypes. And plastic and fiber technologies permit synthesizing of almost anything—from marble to carved wood, from leather to silk— into materials that are far more easily maintained than the real thing.

In selecting both period and style, there are expert guidelines to follow. Just remember to treat them as looks to adapt, rather than to duplicate exactly. No one, except a curator, perhaps, really wants to live a life of museum propriety.

If you want to live Spanish, you'll opt for hand-carved woods boasting a robust aristocratic beauty. French style invites a Louis range from the heavily ornamented and over-scaled manner of Louis XIV to classically masculine forms of Napoleonic times.

Italian decorating imagines itself as gilt-trimmed, inlaid and appliqued. English ranges from the crude, but serviceable Jacobean designs, exemplified by milking stools, monk's benches and trestle tables, to the revivalist designs of Queen Victoria's lengthy reign. Early American was the original eclectic look: a blending of racial origins and tastes, a reflection of our melting-pot heritage. Settlers seeking to recreate the worlds left behind produced useful but unornamented furniture limited to benches, chests, stools and settles. Depending on their origins, their few totally functional accessories might have included pewter tankards

of Dutch or Flemish character, French painted or enameled tole trays, English brass bed warmers. The settler years (1607-1750) produced the cherishable look of honest hand-crafting so envied today.

American Traditional, on the other hand, is an interpretation of more formal and refined Colonial times, dating from 1750. Eclectic decorating refers to an aesthetically pleasing mix of many styles. The key words are "selecting the best," however. Not just any old hodgepodge will do. Which brings us to modern, or contemporary, decorating: a fresh and positive search for original themes, colors, materials, fashions and functions as it relates to today's liberated style of living.

Featured here, four looks from the American past, up-dated. A young ceramic artist living in California effects a lifestyle resembling the simplicity of "mission," a style inspired by the humble way of life of Spanish missionaries in what is now Mexico and the American southwest. Furnishings were confined to a few solid pieces, such as chests, tables and chairs, made to endure. Here, simple wood pieces effect a look of understated strength in a setting of brick and stucco walls. Windows are shuttered, rather than curtained. Accessories are largely pottery. Rich colors are mostly derived from the Spanish fandangos. And art is dictated by emotion, not intellect.

THE AMERICAN PAST UP-DATED

Colonial charm is recreated in a spacious, country-house bedroom, top. A pediment-framed mirror, plus chests and dressers with bail pulls and brass backplates, add full measure of authenticity. Hitchcock chair and canopy bed add romance and nostalgia. Wood plank flooring with toe-warming area rug preserves the past, while a modern urethane finish protects the present.

Country-look dining, center, is a comfortable blend of casual elements borrowed long ago from rural English and French homes. It is a style of rugged natural woods, of barn siding shutters and printed floral wallcoverings, of a free arrangement of furniture: a groaningly large oak table with pedestal base, a quartet of bentwood, cane-seated chairs and a pastry cupboard with pierced tin door panels. Decorating now, as then, insists on practicality. Here, the wall is fabric-like vinyl.

Pine furniture, a look of honest handcrafting that prevailed throughout the 17th and early 18th century, dominates the dining room, bottom. Early English influence asserts itself in the virile cabinet work, heroic-scaled table and rush-seated, ladder-back chairs. Accessories now, as then, are edited down to a few key functional items that work for their place in the home by holding, storing or lighting. Past lamp styles up-dated include the tole chandelier and astral, or oil lamp, now electrically wired.

DESIGN: GILBERT A. GRAY, AID. PHOTOGRAPHY: VAN DERVEER.

ITALIAN, FRENCH AND ENGLISH: ROOTS OF TRADITIONAL

Chances are you're a traditionalist if your preference is a decorating style flavored by another continent, another time, another culture. Even American Traditional has its roots in European cultures, directly reflecting 18th century merchant trade between the Colonies and the Continent. Fruits of this trade: a mix of Oriental porcelains, Flemish brasses and large architectural English furniture such as bookcases and breakfronts bearing neo-classic design details—broken pediments and dentil moldings. Colonists wealthy enough to import furniture borrowed an aristocratic lifestyle from London cabinetmakers such as Hepplewhite, Sheraton, Chippendale and the Brothers Adam. Ultimately, just as today, an indigenous look developed in the hands of native Colonial-born designers.

In the Manhattan apartment, above left, the opulent look of velvet fabrics, typical of the 16th century Italian Renaissance era, is combined with intimately scaled 18th century French furniture. The formal looking room lends itself to informal conversation with props for entertaining secreted in a built-in cabinet wall. Clues to comfort are in seating pieces that include a pair of polite wood-framed armchairs, or bergères, covered in needlepoint brocade, and a modern-day recliner upholstered in brandy velvet. Sumptuously draped windows contribute to the elegant mood.

Witness a fresh interpretation of American Traditional, below left. The look of handwoven fabrics is reproduced in the synthetic plaid and patterned stand-ins upholstering the seating and walls. Furniture pieces follow characteristic traditional design lines: Chippendale camel back sofas, wing chair, Queen Anne desk, butler's tray table, huntboard with Welsh cupboard —all typical of English styles reinterpreted by Colonists. A cozy arrangement of furniture plus bright, cheery colors are responsible for this small room's very special warmth and welcome.

The room below features a far more sophisticated and formal translation of many of the same traditional pieces shown opposite. An adaptation of Traditional styling, it includes the ubiquitous wing chair — originally designed as a hearth-side piece to hoard warmth and ward off drafts—the butler's tray table, Queen Anne desk and secretary-bookcase. Reproductions of fine English furniture carry such design hallmarks, here, as gracefully curved (cabriole) Queen Anne legs, antiqued brass bail pulls and candlestand with tripod leg. Additional style elements include chair-rail molding and Oriental rug.

MODERN DECORATING: WARM-BLOODED AND ORIGINAL

Modern, as a decorating style, relates directly to a search for forms that fulfill functions. There are very few conceits or frivolities in classic modern, although in the fun and passing faddish, an amorphous beanbag or inflatable chair or water bed will show up just often enough to amuse. Good modern offers dynamics in colors, shapes, materials and uses— from super wall graphics to molded urethane to sling seating, sofa beds and modular shelving. Earliest stylings owe a lot to German technologies perfected in the Bauhaus, a school of designers whose use of machine-age materials, like steel, and adherence to strong architectural lines are now considered classic.

Bauhaus is followed by Scandinavian, not just the austere and motel-typical variety, but rather, warm-blooded sculptural designs in hand-rubbed and oiled woods. Good Scandinavian Modern has soft lines with handcrafted appeal.

New Modern includes Milanese —the avant-garde emulating from Italy—soft-edge, undulating, organic shapes with voluptuous curves, many appearing to have no bones, just billowing, cushioned good looks. Molded plastic pieces in circus colors serve multiple purposes. As a style, it's up-to-the-minute and definitely not for the conservative.

American Modern is a blend of all these German, Scandinavian and Italian stylings, artfully combined to create a totally original idiom. It is curved. It is angular. It is mechanical. It blends well and shows great respect for tradition, in fact dipping back into 19th century American Shaker for simple, yet extremely functional designs.

Modern is achieved, below, with Danish-dominated blond woods in a wallfull of modular stacks that hold and show and hide everything from collections to entire stereo systems. There's a great play of textures among the slick woods, cork walls and carpeted, platformed floor.

Right, above, unfurbelowed Shaker designs are purposely set off by neutral colorings and accessorized to a minimum with naturalistic art. Everything does double duty. The trestle table serves as a hobby surface between meals. Spindle-back chairs can double as auxiliary seating in other parts of the home. The buffet server is actually a magazine rack.

The fireplace is still the heart of the modern home (right, below), now surrounded by low sectional seating covered in fabric with plenty of '30s cling. Loose-woven casements allow sunlight to filter in, reflecting off the slick chrome-and-glass cocktail table. The Parsons table, an American original, runs the length of a wall, holding native, yet modern-looking replicas of Indian pottery.

ECLECTIC: "SELECTING" THE "BEST" OF SEVERAL STYLES

DESIGN: ALLISON-REMICK. PHOTOGRAPHY: TAYLOR LEWIS. SOURCE: JOANNE YOUNG.

If Colonial America was eclectic, it was only a modest mix compared with today's liberated, tasteful combining of the best of other cultures into a world-related decorating style. To live eclectically, you throw out the ground rules in favor of an effect that expresses your own highly personal and individual way of life. An arbiter of taste explains eclectic: "If you wish to mix French furniture with Tibetan, you can do it. If you want to use a 20th century vinyl tile floor with an 18th century carpet, you can do it. If you want to upholster a 17th century chair with a 20th century synthetic, you can do it. If you like French Provincial furniture mixed with George II silver mixed with Moroccan carpets, your taste would be considered eclectic." Eclectic is an innovative mingling and mixing of riches of the past with the blessings of the present, editing out the impure and non-classic with discreet abandon. It is more an intuitive than deliberate way of decorating. Its very non-rules invite easy and frequent change, forever guarding against sameness.

Because these rooms are freely styled and reject exclusive interpretations, they could almost be considered contemporary, but instead, they are eclectic. The mix is of both new and old with obvious emphasis on old.

In the dining-kitchen, above left, stalwart furniture was weeded out from among the

awful welter of novelty items that marked the Victorian revival. The era's brocaded wall look is simulated in a pattern-on-pattern vinyl developed 100 years later. Mixed and matching pieces of china are cached in a recess that once housed the ironing board, now fitted with shelves. Brass, glass, silver and pewter candlesticks have their origins in France, England and Scandinavia. A huge old French Provincial armoire that once held a clothes wardrobe, now serves as the pantry; the chest under the window holds linens.

The validity of mixing past with present is proven, below left, in a span of centuries from 18th to 20th, of continents from Europe to the Orient. The bold stroke is in the fauteuil, or Louis XVI cushion-seat, open-arm chair treated to a goldenrod finish, then upholstered in an up-dated turn-of-the-century "art moderne" print. Other anachronisms in any room other than an eclectic one are the Chinese chest topped with Greek urns, an English tea table set with German silver. The totally modern tuxedo-styled sofa is upholstered in totally modern velvet with a protective finish.

In among those several centuries of English styles that most influenced the American colonies is Oriental, expertly interpreted by Thomas Chippendale. The almost pure geometry of Oriental design adapts easily to new American lifestyles. Simple in line, pure in colors and distinguished by linear subtlety, Oriental seems contemporary to our time, mixing gracefully with almost any style of furnishings.

The Oriental-flavored bedroom above is a good example of English Regency decorating, a look of special intimate quality that originated after Chippendale during the George IV years (1795-1820). An exotic use of paisley fabric on the walls with bamboo-trimmed furniture and a Bokara rug suddenly transforms an ordinary suburban home into an extraordinary and worldly one.

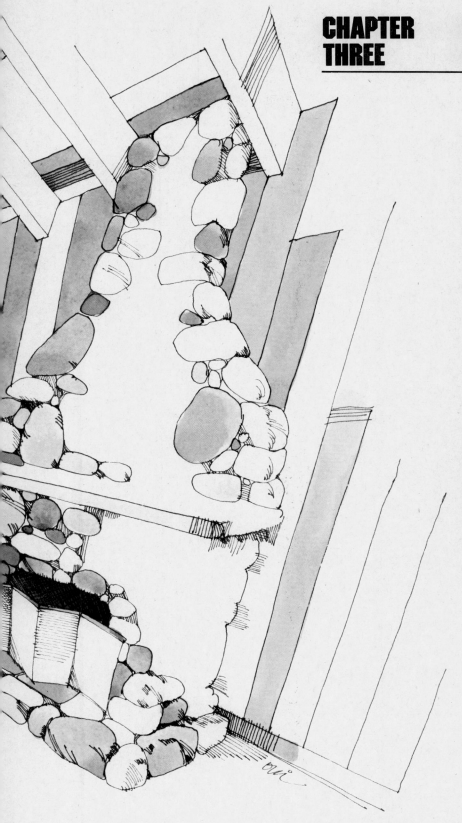

CHAPTER THREE

FLOORS, WALLS AND CEILINGS

Most decorating begins with the floor and works up. Alas, only the privileged few have hardwood flooring. A majority depend on such materials as carpet, vinyl, ceramic tile or paint to unify, define, warm and theme a home.

Function dictates the kind of flooring. Once the need is filled, taste can be indulged through color, pattern and texture of your choice.

Like Everest, walls and ceilings need to be conquered. Luckily the methods for tackling them are far simpler. Paint can shorten or heighten, widen or narrow a room. Mirrors can enlarge or distort. Corrupted old plaster can be camouflaged with wallcoverings. With wood paneling or beams, even the barest walls and ceilings can be architected.

GUIDELINES TO FLOORS, WALLS AND CEILINGS: YOUR STARTING POINTS

Floors, walls and ceilings form the cubes in which we live. Although the walls occupy the largest space, flooring is the element that gets the hardest wear and, therefore, is usually the most expensive of the areas to decorate. As for ceilings, they're all too often neglected when our decorating plans are made and budgeted. Yet, given special consideration, they can be an important element in the overall scheme.

Function and budget are the two most important guidelines for the selection of flooring. Function comes first, and how these guidelines have changed! No longer are we limited to a hard surface in the kitchen, carpeting in the bedroom. That has changed with the introduction of new, non-absorbent fibers in carpet and cushion-back softness in vinyl which feels like carpet underfoot. The choice is broad and almost anything goes, providing it suits the needs of the particular room.

Some rooms, such as those for children, benefit by a combination of flooring types—resilient for games and trains and trucks; soft, like an area rug, for floor sitting and keeping toes warm on wintry nights. Unless wall-to-wall carpeting is your lifelong dream, the same combination can often work well for master or guest bedrooms, family rooms, even a kitchen with its breakfast alcove.

Once the basic choice is made—between hard and soft surface flooring—you will be faced with numerous and confusing "other" considerations. Style and color usually win out provided the price is within the established budget.

However, when making an investment of this size, it behooves you to know something about fiber and construction, or composition, their counterpart in the case of hard surface flooring. Only then will you know what to expect as to performance and care. There are volumes of up-to-date information printed on the subject, available from manufacturers in the flooring industry.

Choosing wallcoverings can be equally confusing. Wallpapers are often some material other than paper. Paneling is seldom what it pretends to be. All in all, it's the look you want for the price you can afford that's your primary consideration.

The breakfast room, below, features the look of barn siding in paneled walls and cabinets. Balancing the vast expanse of dark is a white ceiling, plus red and white vinyl floor tiles in a checkerboard pattern. This motif, in miniature, is repeated in the café curtains.

The wood look on walls is a growing trend in both family rooms and dens, as well as kitchens. Though it's somewhat more expensive than wallpaper or paint, it offers a look of warmth and permanency.

Paneling comes in planks as well

DESIGN: ABBEY DARER, AID. PHOTOGRAPHY: BILL MARGERIN

THE WARMTH OF WOOD ON WALLS AND FLOORS

as in larger, easier-to-work-with panels. Originally paneling was all wood, but now convincing simulations of nearly any wood can be found at much less expense. Some even simulate leather, marble and slate. Others come in colors and designs that are especially suitable for bathrooms.

Wood paneling is also available in antiqued color finishes. The dining nook, above right, is paneled in antiqued blue with a floral-print cotton fabric for its dado and ceiling. Beams are phony ones, made of lightweight polyurethane, that have all the rusticity of the real thing. Applying the fabric between helps to deaden sound, a problem that could also be minimized with acoustical ceiling tiles, now available in a wide variety of textured styles.

Wood, in the form of oak strip flooring, dominates the living room, below. Finished with clear polyurethane, the grain and natural color of the wood are allowed to show through, making it an especially ideal background for Scandinavian-style furnishings. The Flokati rug provides textural contrast, while defining the conversation area.

In the dining room of this restored home, below right, the original wide pine plank floor (hidden under linoleum for decades) was reclaimed, sanded down, sealed and finished to a satin patina with bowling alley wax, proving wall-to-wall wood can have just as much warmth and character as carpeting.

DESIGN: MARY JANE GRAHAM, NSID.
PHOTOGRAPHY: HEDRICH-BLESSING.

DESIGN: LAVERNE FINLEY. PHOTOGRAPHY: EDUARDO LATOUR.

DESIGN: DELPHENE RICHARDS, NSID.
PHOTOGRAPHY: REG VAN CUYLENBERG.

INSTANT MOOD MAKER:
WALLPAPER ON WALLS, CEILINGS

If flooring is the major budget consideration in decorating, then wallpaper is the major mood maker. There's nothing quite so simple or effective as using a patterned wallpaper, or more accurately wallcovering, to establish a room's total scheme. Many styles of wallcovering have companion patterns, some even matching fabric. These further simplify decorating decisions.

Of course, along with setting the style, wallcovering also performs a function. Patterned and textured coverings are slow to show soil and can also be used to camouflage uneven walls. Many are either made of vinyl or vinyl coated to insure washability and durability—especially important in kitchens, baths and rooms that children frequent.

Two patterns are often better than one. The studio, below left, employs coordinated papers in flowers and stripes. The artistic owner painted the floor a warm cocoa brown, then repeated the wall's floral motif in a painted-on "area rug." The money saved on the do-it-herself floor was spent on papering the ceiling.

When two or more patterns are combined, one should be larger in scale than another. Since manufacturers are alert to this fact, you'll find that their style books include numerous companion patterns.

Obviously, the kitchen and entry foyer, below, sport walls that were made for each other—a small check and a floral-on-check, both in brown, white and black. The window frame, arch and foyer dado are painted brown, outlining and defining the two patterns. Notice how kitchen cabinets take on a custom look when framing is painted dark; doors, white.

Scrubbable white vinyl covers the kitchen floor, while the foyer is carpeted brown to discourage soiling and tracking.

DESIGN: PEG WALKER

DESIGN: NANJA WILLIAMS. PHOTOGRAPHY: MARTIN HELFER
LOCATION: LARWIN'S GREENBROOK, CORAM, L.I., N.Y.

Wallcoverings needn't be on the wall to dictate a room's style. A wallpapered ceiling almost guarantees sweet dreams in the bedroom, right. The paper continues a few inches down the wall to meet the window top like a canopy over the entire room.

A second pattern, the green and white check, is used for curtains and quilted spread. Pale green carpet, laid wall-to-wall, visually expands the floor space as does the monochromatic color scheme. Another room expanding ploy: Mirrors on sliding closet doors, floor-to-ceiling and wall-to-wall.

Sometimes a patterned wallcovering is combined with a solid. Although paint might achieve the same visual results, a solid vinyl wallcovering offers extra washability and permanency.

The country kitchen, right, is always in bloom.

Instead of picking up the ordinary background white for shutters and ceiling, apple green vinyl wallcovering in a denim texture was selected. The effect is cozy and warm all year long.

Beams were improvised out of stock lumber, first heavily "distressed" with hammer and nail, then painted white and nailed in place to outline walls, ceiling and window, carrying out the country theme. Apricot carpeting was chosen, rather than the expected green. Note window shade covered to match walls.

DESIGN: BIC JONSON, NSID. PHOTOGRAPHY: LEWIS STUDIO.

NATURAL MATERIALS VERSUS
THE GREAT PRETENDERS

There's something about materials such as brick, stone, marble and tile that give substance to a room. As building materials, they've been in use for hundreds of years. Their use today evokes visions of country kitchens, Mediterranean villas and crenelated castles.

Because of their expense, these materials have always been in somewhat limited use. But, thanks to modern-day technology, you can now enjoy their look at a fraction of the cost of the real thing. The look of tile and brick, marble and stone, slate and stucco, and numerous others, has been simulated on such popular and inexpensive materials as self-adhesive vinyl paper, vinyl flooring and even carpeting, not to mention light-weight plastic "bricks" and "stones" that you can mortar yourself!

Witness the family room, left, above. What was once an architecturally uninteresting room achieves distinction with a wall of brick, albeit make-believe. A few yards of self-adhesive, brick-imprinted vinyl paper do the trick at a very modest cost.

Although brick walls usually bring to mind fruitwood and other country furnishings, they mate equally as well with modern. Low budget furnishings include: A Parsons table, purchased in the raw, now vinyl clad in a new extra-strength, extra-width self-adhesive paper that's especially suited to table-tops and other areas of hard knocks; director's chairs, upholstered in tortoise print vinyl; and a felt-type indoor-outdoor carpet. Modular bookshelf units house not only books, but also games and stereo equipment that encourage family members to gather there frequently.

There's nothing like the real thing, of course, and many a homemaker is willing to give up something else in return for a brick fireplace or a true country kitchen. The one, left, below, was considered a worthwhile investment by the family that lives and spends most of its time there. The walls are brick; the floor, a rich terra cotta ceramic tile.

Dark hardwood cabinets are in keeping with the traditional atmosphere, as are the furniture

and stained shutters. The stucco ceiling is equally authentic with its hand-hewn beams.

Another budget "pretender" is self-stick vinyl floor tile, available in patterns to simulate everything from Delft to Spanish tile, from marble to mosaic, from wood to brick. Of special interest in this category are the adhesive-backed tiles that you can install yourself, thus avoiding the high cost of installation.

Close your eyes and try to imagine the sophisticated dining area, below, without its bright Mediterranean "tiled" floor. It wouldn't be quite the same. You can duplicate this mellow, old-world look in your own home in just one afternoon—with 12", self-stick vinyl tiles.

The unique wall treatment consists of red felt panels—which act as poster art mats—against white painted walls. Folding screens from an old mansion divide dining area from entryway.

The choice of pattern in carpeting and carpet squares today is almost as wide as in resilient flooring. The living room, below right, is floored in a sophisticated geometric print carpet made of individual latex foam-backed carpet squares. The pattern makes joining of the seams less obvious. The choice between "hard" or "soft" flooring today is based not so much on price or pattern, but more on personal preference for the feel of the material underfoot. Almost the same look can be achieved by either.

PHOTOGRAPHY: PAULUS LEESER.

THE CUSTOM TOUCH OF CREATIVE COMBINATIONS

Of all the decorating tools, color is the least expensive, yet probably the most valuable. Dark colors on walls and floors can make a room seem smaller while white or pastels seem to expand a vista. Patterns that are large in scale or highly contrasting in color are usually best stretched out over large spaces, while smaller-scaled, more subtly colored schemes work better in small rooms or, at least, in rooms for small members of the family.

Dens and studies quite frequently have dark walls to project an atmosphere of quiet contemplation. In a bedroom, dark walls are conducive to relaxation. Deep forest green walls in a master bedroom/sitting area, left, provide a dramatic background for print draperies, Roman shade and seat cushion. A second pattern dominates the floor by way of a 12′ geometric broadloom carpet, custom bordered with strips of shag left over from another room.

Just as dark colors are considered masculine or restful, so are light ones viewed as feminine or blithesome. The sewing center with its wallpaper in green, yellow, pink and white plaid is cheerful and bright. Carpeting is nylon in a two-tone green plushy shag; furniture is lacquered yellow. This same scheme could work equally well in a dining room or young girl's bedroom.

Mixing patterns and colors artfully takes careful planning. Selecting a neutral palette is one method of insuring success. The living room directly below is a harmonious mix of black, brown and white with one gold chair as an accent. The plaid carpet inspired the scheme. The brown is repeated in dark painted walls and subtle brown/black pattern beneath a white chair rail. A mostly white rya rug on the carpet lends a custom, room-lighting touch.

Vibrant color combinations are usually best reserved for rooms, such as bedrooms or baths, that are used infrequently or during short waking hours. Hot pink, marigold and orange are combined in the bedroom, bottom right. The wallpaper zigzags in hot pink and orange, striped with silver. White beams have been added for architectural interest. The orange shag carpet, wall-to-wall, balances the stucco-textured ceiling, painted marigold.

PHOTOGRAPHY: PAULUS LEESER.

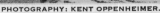

PHOTOGRAPHY: KENT OPPENHEIMER.

SMALL SPACES
TURNED SPECTACULAR

The greater the decorating challenge, the greater the potential for a spectacular solution. That's one optimist's way of looking at things. That little area you rejected as a lost cause, or merely neglected, might turn out to be the showplace of your home if given a little attention.

An entryway, kitchen, bath or back hall can be the stage upon which you try out your decorating wings—experimenting with a costly material you wouldn't dare consider in a larger quantity, or picking a pattern or color combination you might hesitate to confront guests with in the living room.

A kitchen is a wonderful place to

begin. Since you spend so much time there, you certainly deserve pleasant surroundings. The problem of a long, narrow kitchen with its small, windowless breakfast area has been cheerfully solved, below, with floor and wall interest. A small-scale geometric-printed carpet was installed wall-to-wall to

unify the two areas. Its pattern disguises most crumbs and spills until they can be vacuumed or sponged away.

Bees in an organized swarm dot the wallpaper, also patterned small in scale so as not to be overpowering. A row of pictures on the wall gives the eye visual

DESIGN: DAVE FARRAR. PHOTOGRAPHY: VINCENT LISANTI. LOCATION: SOUTH COMMONS, CHICAGO.

relief. Another space-making ploy: A clear, glass-top table that takes up the absolute minimum of visual space.

In kitchens, per se, pattern is usually confined to the floor, since wall-hung cabinets will break up the drama of all but the smallest wallpaper patterns. In bathrooms and foyers, however, interesting wall treatments are the rule rather than the exception, inviting experimentation.

What can possibly be inspiring about a small hall or entryway? One clever woman found the solution for her hallway's cracked and impossible wall at a local building supply store. Inexpensive corrugated sheet aluminum now not only covers her problem wall, above right, but creates a dazzling backdrop for a collection of framed art. The artwork on the floor: A graphic rya rug.

A more conservative, yet still innovative, spectacular is exemplified by the totally coordinated kitchen, below right. One sunshine yellow pattern covers all—walls, floor, even windows and seat cushions. Believe it or not, this flooring is vinyl—a new cushioned sheet material that combines the look and feel of carpet underfoot with the damp-mop practicality of resilient flooring. Washable wallpaper and matching cotton fabric—available by the yard—are added to make a happy trio. This total coordination guarantees almost foolproof decorating.

WALL TREATMENTS FOR SPECIAL EFFECTS

Anyone with a desire for different kinds of backgrounds is in luck these days. The choices are inspiring and limitless, ranging from conventional colors and patterns in wallcoverings to uncoy dramatic designs. Capitalizing on the chameleon properties of vinyls, walls can assume cork, stone, marble and brick looks without costly installations.

Several strong patterns can be combined in one room. Ticking, leopard prints and supergraphics are fashionable now where they once would have been thought freakish. Old bricks are in, damasks have been revived in contemporary black-and-white as well as traditional colors. Even tapestry-like fabric walls are possible because of both simplified application techniques and a finishing process that makes them resistant to dirt, stain and moisture.

Another device for breaking up the monotony of a large expanse of walls is artificial architecture: Cardboard panels and moldings that imitate plaster work, lightweight dimensional beams that can be glued into place, strategically placed paneling and mirrors.

Paint contrasted or matched with materials also serves simply and well. Contrast is achieved, opposite, top left, with one wall papered and the bed wall shingled—an inexpensive technique involving shingles from a building supply dealer, nailed on straight or at random. The room is predominantly green, naturally themed to the wood shingled wall.

A monochromatic room, opposite, top right, is architected by its two-toned red wall, accomplished by masking off the desired zigzag pattern, then painting.

Matching wallpaper and fabric are used to create a focal point bedroom wall, opposite, bottom left. This bold use, in a small space, of a dramatic-color floral is set off by totally neutral carpeting.

A beamed cathedral ceiling makes the room opposite, bottom right, architecturally outstanding to begin with. To accentuate that detailing, the walls are given individual attention: The headboard wall is covered in a screen-printed damask-patterned wallpaper. The other walls are painted stark white, one becoming a foil for an arrangement of art.

Walls, below, were designed into the house plan and kept beautifully simple, except for one pine wood carving surrogating for a headboard. Built into the side of a mountain, the bedroom of this home has a tree house feel. Rough, native Ponderosa pine walls and ceiling were spray painted to match the natural color of the wool carpeting. Color accent is the jewel-tone red-orange bedspread.

DESIGN: DICK KNECHT. PHOTOGRAPHY: KEN NORGARD.

CHAPTER FOUR

WINDOW TREATMENTS

Since old Norse days, windows have kept their meaning in the home—as an outlet for the eye, inlet for light and air. Modern ingenuity adds fashion to function, making windows also beautiful to the beholder. Function is enhanced by imaginative combinations of curtains, shades, shutters, blinds, you-name-it.

Certain treatments can also disguise flaws. Sheers or shojis help obscure bad views, fuzzing their outlines, preserving privacy.

Café curtains hung on the wall between sill and floor effect windows to the floor (left); tieback side draperies literally frame a good view. In any case, with a little creative thought, windows can become a room's supreme harmonizer, as interesting to look at, as out.

GUIDELINES TO WINDOWS: FUNCTIONAL AND FASHIONABLE

By following a few simple rules of thumb, it is possible to make windows not only the first thing you see on entering a room, but also the best. Treatments can have influence on selection of both furnishings and color schemes. Wood panels or shutters, for example, radiate warmth, comfort and a feeling of permanency. Decorative cornices and swag draperies help to create a period formality. Café curtains set a cozy, informal mood. Ruffled tiebacks generally go well with Provincial or Colonial styles. Grilles give a Mediterranean feel. Casements lean toward Contemporary. Shojis establish Oriental serenity.

You can begin with the windows and plan the rest of the room accordingly, keeping in mind these general rules: Textured materials tend to soften a large area. Sheers help to emphasize architectural details. Patterns act as catalysts in relating windows to other fabrics in the room, and are best used in large rooms rather than small ones. Plain curtains or draperies should be used in a room that has patterned upholstery. Window shades help add dimension to plain windows. Blinds tend to tidy up windows with many small panes of glass. Austrian shades soften harsh window lines. Curtains and draperies coordinated to the wallpaper help to unify a room. Vertical shades heighten the look of windows. Shutters help to frame good views, block out bad ones. Valances or cornices

should be avoided in a low-ceilinged room, on an extremely wide expanse of windows or with floor-to-ceiling windows.

Windows with a good view are best treated with restraint. Most curtain and drapery treatments are simply gilding the lily. However, to control light, air and privacy, shades, shutters and even plants are useful.

Windows with bad views are easily disguised by vertical blinds, some curtain treatments, beads, grilles, shojis and countless other techniques that help integrate them into the room, detracting from the outside. The same techniques can be utilized not only to improve a bad view or balance unbalanced windows, but also to conceal obstructive architectural elements such as wall juts, radiators and air-conditioners.

Finally, certain window products, such as scrim-weight shades, not only enhance a window, but also reduce the intensity of strong summer sun. And heavyweight draw draperies help baffle sound, while adding an aesthetic plus to a room.

An old-fashioned concept is revived, right, to restore the essence of ladylike to a circa 1900 farmhouse bedroom. A shirred and ruffled heading overlays a cascading Austrian shade—both home sewn in humble bleached muslin. Ladylike prints cover walls and plumpy chintz chair. Everything is suitably Victorian in scale.

A bay window, right, is framed with drapery panels and gracefully shaped cornice. Glass curtains provide privacy while allowing light to filter through.

Tieback draperies fashioned of printed sheets, far right, team with sheers to dress outwardly swinging casement windows. A brazen geometric, also a sheet, upholsters the box springs and simulates a headboard stapled around plywood padded with fiberfill. These sheets have a fabric protector finish making them particularly suitable for decorating projects.

An ideal treatment, right, bottom, for the sliding-door window wall is pinch-pleated draperies, here given a custom look with harmonizing traverse rod, chains and holdbacks in antiqued brass.

A small window, far right, bottom, is visually enlarged by its painted-on, contrasting color border. Simple shirred curtains with ball-fringe-trimmed tiebacks repeat the wall color.

CURTAINS
AND DRAPERIES

DESIGN: VIRGINIA CHAPPELL. PHOTOGRAPHY: EVERETTE SHORT.

N: GEORGE MAHONEY. PHOTOGRAPHY: HEDRICH-BLESSING.

DESIGN: EDMUND MOTYKA. PHOTOGRAPHY: PAULUS LEESER.

DESIGN: NANJA WILLIAMS. PHOTOGRAPHY: MARTIN HELFER.
LOCATION: LARWIN'S GREENBROOK, CORAM, L.I., N.Y.

DESIGN: MALCOLM SCHACTER.

DESIGN: RAY KINDELL, AID.

SHUTTERS, SHOJIS
AND USEFUL COMBINATIONS

A window treatment is rarely executed with a single element, be it a shade, shutter or curtain. A combination of elements is usually needed to best service both function and appearance.

City windows facing more in than out can be disguised by shojis or other translucent sliding panels. Sky "blight" is obscured, opposite, top, by something serenely Oriental—a decorative wood frame onto which silky, light-filtering polyester fabric has been stretched. The right-hand panel slides left on ready-made, concealed shoji tracks for an occasional breath of fresh air and a glimpse beyond. Few curtain or drapery treatments would better serve the purpose of letting in light, shutting out sight.

Minimal furnishings are softly shaped and loudly colored to stand out like sculpture against the white of the windows, the plum of the rug. Low platform seating poised by tall, graceful

DESIGN: JULIE DENISON AND RAY KINDELL, AID.

potted plants fulfills the serene scene.

The window wall, opposite, bottom, of a one-room apartment in an old townhouse receives special decorative emphasis from a handsome shade-and-shutter combination.

Laminated window shades and valances repeat the exquisite crewelwork of the studio couch and love seat. The shades are framed with white, double-hung shutters, the bottom pair closed to discreetly conceal an unsightly air-conditioner in one window. Everywhere, both inherited and collected furnishings are subtly interrelated so that each portion of the room produces its own vignette.

Shades and café curtains, below, left, collaborate to turn a blah kitchen window into a focal point. The window is dressed with a chevron print in bright, sunlit colors that cheer year-round, rain or shine. The shade is a do-it-yourself project. You

can fashion a custom shade from any closely woven, average-weight fabric simply by ironing it onto a special heat-activated adhesive-coated shade cloth. The café curtains were made out of matching cotton. The tablecloth, in canary yellow edged with green gimp and orange fringe, carries through the color scheme.

Where some period rooms are modernized through window design, the modern condominium bedroom, below right, has been given period flavor by its window treatment. Great restraint has been exerted to avoid overdoing the look. The tailored treatment features a wide Roman shade—a horizontally pleated, rather than shirred, variation on the Austrian shade—in fabric to match wallcovering around and below. White floor-to-ceiling draw draperies flank shade on either side. White Provincial furniture and shag carpeting are a dramatic background for the floral print.

DESIGN: DERRELL BENEFIELD. PHOTOGRAPHY: EVERETTE SHORT.

49

VERSATILE-PURPOSE WINDOW SHADES

DESIGN: PEG WALKER.

Fun and games flourish in this low-budget attic room with its difficult dormer window. A window shade, framed by painting the recess a contrasting color, solves the problem and provides an adjustable view revealing sun and sky when raised, or cutting a swath of lemon, white and tangerine stripes in the ceiling, something like a master canvas, when lowered. It was created of a remnant, laminated to shade cloth by the iron-on method.

Colors are repeated in toss pillows, built-in day-bed cover and vinyl-clad chairs. Everything is easy care and pillow covers come off for dunking in warm suds or automatic washer.

DESIGN: MARION GARDINER-STUDIN, NSID.

DESIGN: PEG WALKER.

Scrim-weight shades, opposite, bottom left, chosen to suit the architecture of sliding glass panels, help to shield the strong glare of sunlight, while allowing a see-through view to the outside. They are also marvelous insulators: Against heat in the summer, cold in the winter. Over-scaled daisy vinyl wallcovering and pebble-patterned vinyl flooring relate the dining area to the outdoors.

A dining room, opposite, right, is sun-controlled through the use of translucent, glass-fiber shade cloth with a hand woven look. The shade pulls down over the sliding glass doors to cut glare and protect privacy, rolls up easily for entrance and exit. It is hung reverse roll in a shadowbox frame, painted white to match the self-adhesive trim. The balance of the room setting includes wallcovering in an oak-grained print and vinyl flooring, both scrubbable and carefree. Bright lemon stacking plates, lime linen napkins and plants help orchestrate a happy conservatory mood.

Corner windows, directly right, in a traditional bed/sitting room feature a combination of draperies with low tiebacks and deep blue shades with tassel pulls and white border trim—a formal complement to the floral of the chintz chairs and wallpaper that establishes the elegant mood and color scheme. Who wouldn't want to breakfast or pen a letter there?

DESIGN: DOROTHY PAUL, FAID.

DESIGN: DERRELL BENEFIELD. PHOTOGRAPHY: EVERETTE SHORT

DISGUISING BAD VIEWS AND PRESERVING PRIVACY

Perhaps the greatest challenge to creative imagination is making something out of nothing. Windows with no view are particularly demanding. And yet for every problem, there are probably at least a dozen solutions to help you make the most of any situation you may encounter in your home.

It's often possible to work within the structure, enlarging and enhancing it. The sheerest casements hung wall-to-wall, opposite, let in light without exposing the non-view. Then, to add interest, white painted latticework has been added. This room features parquet flooring, chocolate brown rug and toast-colored furniture.

A city apartment's dead-end window, opposite, bottom left, is incorporated into the living scheme with the simple addition of prefabricated shutters, louvered for ventilation and light control. Flattering walls are covered in a pale, swirling patterned vinyl that's easily wiped free of city soot.

In the modest studio living room, opposite, bottom right, shutters with fabric inserts architect a large window, obliterate street sights and tie windows closely to the rest of the room. Wood-looking vinyl is a particularly good choice for walls that jut here and there. Key low-budget furnishings include a day-bed/sofa, storage trunk/coffee table, director's chairs, multi-use Parsons table.

Vertical blinds, top right, hide short, unevenly spaced windows, as well as the heating unit and air-conditioner. Blinds were installed with a do-it-yourself system that includes ceiling and chain bottom tracks that control direction of blinds.

Made of window-shade cloth, the vertical "slats" come rolled up in strips that you cut to desired length, then clip taut between tracks. For graphic interest, a few black strips were interspersed among the white.

Graphics are continued throughout the room in the orange-yellow-white geometric area rug, cotton zebra print sofa and row of white cube chests that store books and magazines.

Clever and careful preplanning put visual interest into viewless picture windows, below, bottom. The glass expanse was simply curtained off with strings of shimmering beads, almost imperceptibly in motion, changing reflections with the day and night lighting.

Created by a retired jewelry maker over a decade ago, prestrung beaded curtains are now sold ready to be cut to desired length and inserted by hand, strand by strand, into their own rod. The bookshelves here were built in, not only to supply bonus storage space, but to frame, unify and contain beaded windows.

PHOTOGRAPHY: O. PHILIP ROEDEL.

ENHANCING
INTERESTING VIEWS

Windows with good views can well afford to be decorated by their architecture and as a result, they'll look as good from the outside looking in as from the inside looking out. In addition to shojis, shutters, curtains, draperies, blinds, grilles and trellises, there are other techniques used by those who wish to take special advantage of their view. These include bare windows, or nothing. And, while it sounds ludicrous, nothing sometimes takes more skill and creative imagination than the more conventional methods.

Recognizing intrinsic beauty in the structure of windows, as well as in their relationship to both indoors and out, calls for either the judgment of an artist or the innocence of an amateur. Amateurs sometimes simply luck onto a good thing, a window with a view that demands little or nothing in the way of treatment.

The family room of a suburban home, right, was planned around its occupants' needs, leaving nature to elaborate on the view. Focal point of the room is the corner of glass, subtly framed with floor-to-ceiling shutters that unobtrusively fold against and blend into the wall, allowing the greenery outside to meld with an indoor garden of an 8' rubber tree and tiny rooting plants. The table situated here serves for everything from dining to clay modeling. Accessories include a collective use of original young art and colored yarn that drips down like

Spanish moss from wooden pegs on the wall. The brick flooring bears up bravely under the artless abuses of time.

A dozen clear plastic plant pots filled with herbs ranging from basil to rosemary are perched on acrylic plastic shelves in the "plainest Jane" kitchen window, below right. Shelving is supported by four lengths of brass chains purchased at the local hardware store. The plant print on the wall was cut from fabric yardage and framed.

The best of both worlds mix, opposite, top, in an apartment with a beautiful cityscape. The owners soften the outlook by playing natural plants against man-made skyscraper horizons. Vertical shade-cloth blinds and window sill inlaid with impervious ceramic tile conspire in the plot to enhance.

A bare treatment, opposite, bottom left, enhances the window-seated bay in one end of a living room. Window molding, painted a dark, contrasting color, frames the view as though it were some Rousseau jungle scape. A corner full of plants on plastic pedestals further brings in the outdoor feeling.

Like old-time porch awnings, fabric shades, opposite, bottom right, are drawn up to indulge this walled-in-windows room in nature's light and sights. At nightfall, shades roll down to protect privacy. Furniture consists of a collection of "found" pieces, all made to match with a coat of fresh paint.

CHAPTER FIVE

FURNITURE ARRANGEMENT

No matter what size a home is, it isn't livable unless the space is utilized for maximum comfort and convenience. And the great common denominator of that space is furniture arrangement.

The barny country place with more windows than walls and the boxy city apartment with more walls than windows are both decorating disasters if seating is lined up like ducks in a row around walls, leaving a great anonymous arena of space in the center.

Consider, instead, working from the center of the room out. A sofa, console table or étagère can help divide large space into useful activity areas. Seating can be angled or clustered to induce conversation. Try an unconventional arrangement; it will serve you well.

GUIDELINES TO FURNITURE ARRANGEMENT

Keep in mind the purpose of a room and place individual pieces of furniture where they can serve most conveniently. Don't let anything interfere with traffic patterns in or through a room. Avoid blocking doorways, windows, heating and air-conditioning. Relate arrangements within the room to the architectural features (or lack of them). Try balancing high and low pieces of furniture for a smart mix of both, and in relation to fixed elements in the room, such as high windows.

Trust the modern theory that "less is more," at least to start with. Distribute furniture evenly to avoid over-crowding or under-furnishing. Select furniture to suit the scale of the room. Small rooms generally enjoy small scaled, refined furniture. Large rooms accept more robust pieces.

Dare to disrupt the safe, often boring look of parallels by positioning furniture on a perpendicular or diagonal. And remember: The smaller the room, the more obvious the need for few pieces and the more limited the arrangement. The larger the room, the more freedom for convenient and studied compositions.

The rectangular room, below, offers a wonderful opportunity to divide space into both living and dining areas. The super-simple device is a gorgeous Country French sofa, backed up by a "dough-box" style table that doubles as an auxiliary serving surface. Living is oriented to the fireplace wall, with paired chairs facing each other and accommodated by excellent end tables and reading lights. There's sanity in symmetry when a large focal point wall like this one is involved.

The opposite wall (see floor plan, right), bears a big breakfront with great grace. The confrontation with so much orderly space has been well handled by keeping it open and separated, yet related.

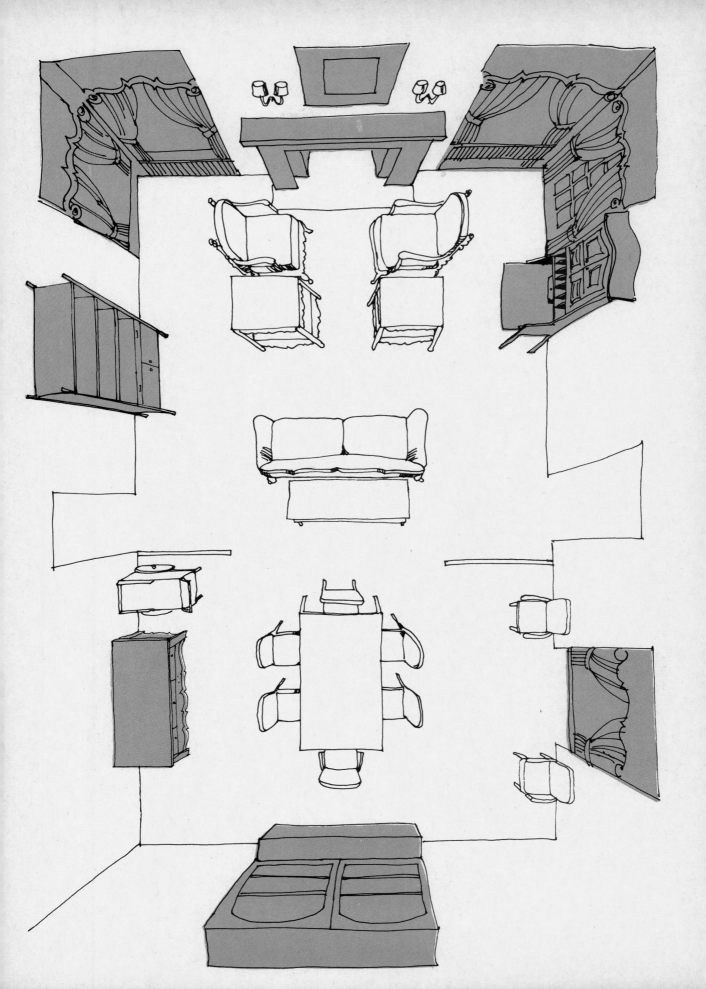

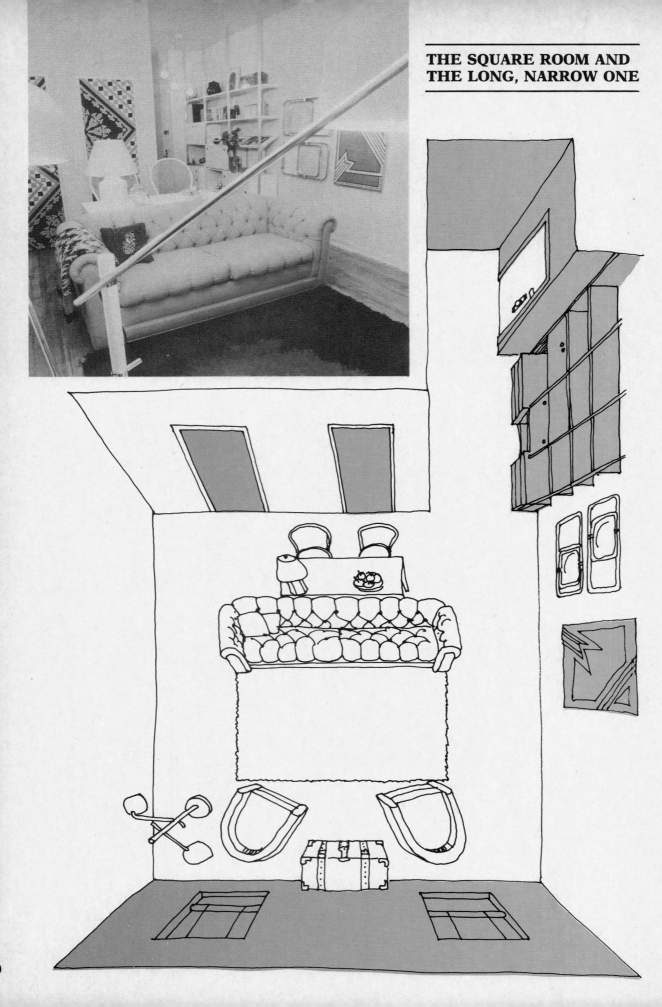

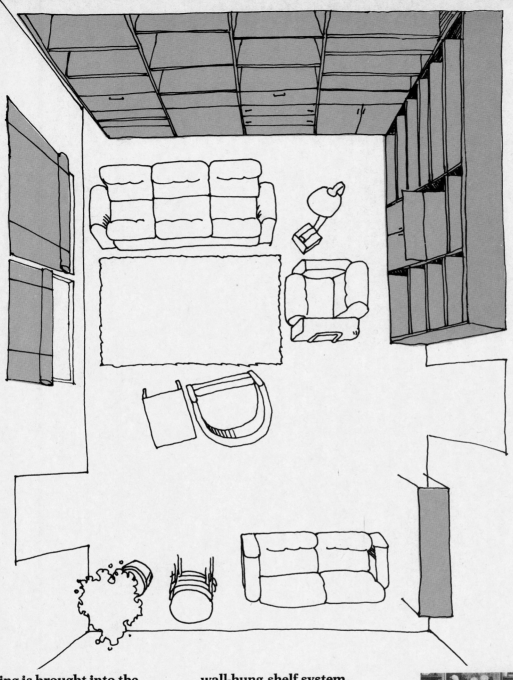

Living is brought into the center of space, left , with seating grouped conveniently around an area rug so that the sofa can be opened for sleeping without moving any other furniture. The table can be used for dining or as a desk. Paired lightweight molded plastic armchairs are arranged to face into conversation without obscuring view. Storage is consigned to a graceful wall-hung shelf system.

A corner-hugging shelf system architects one end of a long, narrow room, right and above. Sofa and chairs, grouped around an area rug, are placed perpendicular to the window wall to create an illusion of width. Love seat and cocktail table in opposite corner provide extra seating without interfering with traffic flow from door to door.

DESIGN: JUDITH GURA. PHOTOGRAPHY: PAULUS LEESER.

MAKING THE MOST OF
THE UBIQUITOUS "L"

In the well-balanced "L," above and right, height is established with rattan stacking chests on the end wall. A love seat backed by a console table maintains a low look where it counts—upon entering—and creates the feeling of a foyer where none exists.

Chairs are worked into the conversational grouping on a space-saving diagonal. Each seating piece is sufficiently lighted for reading and attended by a table surface within arm's reach. Party table and chairs serve for games, as well as for snacking.

Folding screens (see floor plan, right) help to give dining "L" the feeling of a separate room.

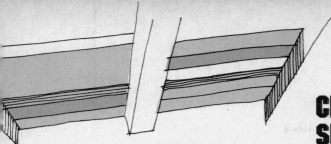

CHAPTER SIX

STORAGE IDEAS

Always a saver, man finds his need for good storage increases as living space diminishes. So ingenuity must compensate. Stacking cabinets, wall-hung shelving and pole systems come to the rescue, rounding corners and dividing space, hoarding the overflow of active family life.

Good organization doubles the capacity of closets. Furniture design itself aids the needy. Witness the floor-standing armoire or clothes wardrobe, the durable brass-cornered campaign chest, the Dutch cupboard that nestles into a corner, bunk beds with trundle blanket chests, the honeycomb wine rack that stacks a dozen bottles—of anything. Bonus over built-ins: You can take them along when you move.

GUIDELINES TO STORAGE: TO SHOW OR CONCEAL

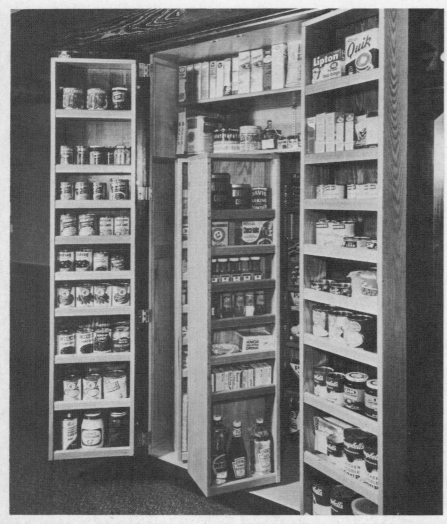

Savers require better organization and more ingenuity than non-savers. There are two basic ways to handle storage problems: (1) build in and conceal, or (2) build out and reveal.

A ready-made chef's pantry, left, has a pivoting center unit that conceals mops and brooms behind canned goods. Spice shelves, below left, turn cabinet door into useful space; a special sliding-door unit adds storage between cabinet and counter. A "found" and restored cabinet, below right, now hoards liquor and silverware.

Pegboard turns the inside of a cabinet door into handy hang-up space, top right. At far right, top, plywood shelves partitioned into cubes store linens and vanity needs. Four well-planned feet of space, opposite, bottom left, contain portable washer and dryer, plus linen shelves. A kitchen pantry, opposite, bottom right, conceals a trash compactor, plus laundry aids on adjustable shelves. Clip-on hooks hold mops and brooms off the floor.

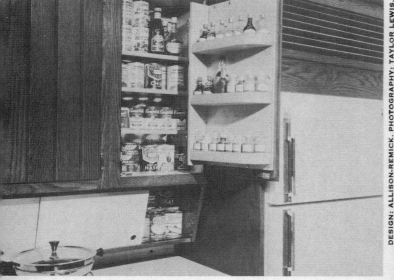

DESIGN: ALLISON-REMICK. PHOTOGRAPHY: TAYLOR LEWIS.

PHOTOGRAPHY: VINCENT LISANTI.

DESIGN: EDMUND MOTYKA. PHOTOGRAPHY: TOM YEE.

FURNITURE DESIGNED FOR STORAGE

Storage wall, left, is composed of assorted plastic cubes, stacked atop a pair of file cabinets. Opposite, bottom: Sewing and all its clutter is an open-and-shut case with a magnificent store-it-all cabinet that opens out to reveal nooks for everything from pins to patterns to fabric, plus sewing machine and table.

Ready-made case unit, right, stores not only linen, china and tableware, but the table itself, which folds away between meals. The modular storage system, below, features European styling that provides a choice of interchangeable units, including drawers, doors and shelves, even a bar and a pull-down dining table. Each piece is finished on all sides so it can be used for dividing space while storing sundries, for living, dining and family room activities.

Ready-made distressed pine cabinetry, below right, is built in to turn a corner into a capacious place for books and desk needs.

69

Rough-sawn random planking is used, left, to create storage bases for beds. A headboard wall with sliding doors triples capacity. Unwasted understair space, below left, stows television and stereo equipment behind panel doors. Below right: Louvered window shutters hide storage on lower shelves of a built-in bookcase unit. Inexpensive and attractive wicker baskets hold small clutter within reach, yet out of sight.

Supergraphic panels in the dining room, top right, are actually doors concealing floor-to-ceiling cabinets—an especially neat trick for coping with lots of clutter in a small space.

Seersucker-paneled cabinet-and-headboard wall, bottom right, stores not only all bedroom necessities, but the Murphy bed itself by day. Alcove curtains and quilted coverlet are fashioned of the same carefree polyester/cotton fabric.

DESIGN: ABBEY DARER, AID. PHOTOGRAPHY: BILL MARGARIN.

DESIGN: SHIRLEY REGENDAHL.

DESIGN: SHIRLEY REGENDAHL.

71

CHAPTER SEVEN

LIGHTING: FOR MOOD AND FUNCTION

Lighting is a home's cosmetic. Good lighting, like good makeup, creates moods, aids functions, affects colors, exaggerates effects.

Lighting comes in all colors, shapes and sizes—from table-top to built-in. It's not just a matter of lamps, shades and bulbs. Fluorescent strips serve a kitchen well; incandescent bulbs, a bathroom. Spotlights dispel shadows. Candlelight transfigures them.

In pleasantly numb surroundings, there will be a combination of low-wattage lamps, built-ins and, perhaps, candles. In crisp and efficient places, you'll find directional lights, such as spots. However you decorate, lighting articulates the scheme.

GUIDELINES TO LIGHTING: FOR BOTH SIGHT AND ATMOSPHERE

Lighting and decorating go hand-in-hand according to experts. Some of it is for setting a mood, some of it is purely for function. Both kinds of lighting are vital to preplanning a home.

Robert Sonneman, an expert who specializes in "putting out the dark," lends these tips: Light a living room according to its many purposes. For a conversation area, softly dimmed light is relaxing. Try dropping a small spot directly over the table serving the conversation area. If the room has pictures on the walls, show them to advantage by flood and spotlighting, which at the same time produces indirect illumination for the rest of the room.

Try direct ceiling light or a curving arc lamp at the game table. Use a large chandelier over a big dining table, but equip it with a dimmer for more informal, romantic entertaining. Supplement the chandelier with wall sconces for interesting distribution of light.

Bedrooms can accommodate both mood lighting and functional spots, the latter placed in the center of the wall about 30" above the mattress. Easily directed away from each other, Mr. Sonneman calls them a potential "marriage saver."

The bathroom or dressing room deserves sunlight or its best artificial substitute, the bright, incandescent source: Small frosted bulbs around the make-up mirror or frosted glass globes flanking the dressing table.

Reading areas call for good and even lighting. The proper desk lamp is an asset to the desk worker, but should be supplemented with overall indirect light. If you are a sprawler, make sure you have a lamp that can sprawl with you.

Remember, a lamp is an appliance that lights your environment. (1) The use of both direct and indirect lighting creates interest and drama in a room. (2) Dimmer controls can vary the mood from bright and formal to relaxed and intimate. (3) Good reading lights combine both direct and indirect light.

To plan lighting in advance of decorating, draw a floor plan, indicate the large functional areas, lay out the furniture, then light the situations for their intended functions. Essentially, a light's primary function is to visually increase the sense of a

space and to change the use of space. It is a very personal thing adding comfort, efficiency, color and variety.

Indirect lighting, below, bounces light from a lower source off a reflective ceiling surface. Direct chandelier light, opposite, top, is equipped with a dimmer switch to vary the dining mood. A table lamp, bottom left, with its three-way bulb, serves to illuminate the table when it is used as a desk, as well as to establish lighting and mood for dining. T-squared Parsons tables fill both work and entertainment demands easily.

The ubiquitous floor lamp that goes anywhere to light everything functions, bottom right, to specifically assist the home typist at his portable table. Lighting for the family room in general is supplied by overhead panels of recessed fluorescents.

PHOTOGRAPHY: DAVE SAGARIN.

DESIGN: HARRIET SCHOENTHAL. PHOTOGRAPHY: EVERETTE SHORT.

SUPER-FUNCTIONAL LIGHTING FOR KITCHENS AND BATHROOMS

A combination of shower spotlights and theatrical soffit lights both glamorize and functionalize a bath/dressing room, far left. In this room, above all, personal needs come vitally into play. The man must be able to shave comfortably, the woman must be able to apply her makeup. The row of frosted 25-watt globe lights does the trick.

Kitchens, the heart of so many homes, should be lighted aesthetically without sacrificing function. A lovely tole lamp, left, brings direct light and beauty to a functional work counter. The lamp is supplemented by overhead fluorescents that indirectly illuminate the entire kitchen area.

Good general lighting for the bathroom, opposite, bottom, is supplied by a luminous dropped ceiling over the sink/vanity. Fluorescents above textured translucent panels dispel shadows and diffuse the light. Wall-to-wall mirrors in the vanity recess tend to enlarge the look of the space and are far superior for seeing than dinky little mirrors over each sink bowl would be.

A kitchen, below left, enjoys overall illumination from a suspended ceiling of translucent panels with two rows of fluorescent tubes above. A light in the range hood provides direct lighting for the cooking center.

In the combination kitchen/family room, below right, several kinds of lighting are used, all to functional advantage. Ceiling fluorescents supply indirect and general light, concealed under-cabinet fixtures provide direct light for counter work surfaces, and a working kerosene lamp adds useful whimsy to the family room.

PHOTOGRAPHY: VINCENT LISANTI.

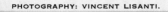

PHOTOGRAPHY: KENT OPPENHEIMER.

SUPER-GLAMOROUS LIGHTING: FOR DINING IN AND OUT

DESIGN: JOSEPHINE SOKOLSKI, PHOTOGRAPHY: STANLEY SHIRE.

"Consider for a moment that you are entering a restaurant," Robert Sonneman invites. "You are with someone you are very fond of and you select a dimly lighted booth in the corner. You gaze at each other through the flicker of a burning candle. The moment belongs to you. There may be 200 people in that restaurant, but the two of you are quite alone. Suddenly lights are ablaze. You are startled. You become unpleasantly aware of the other people. Your moment is gone. All because a busboy hit the switch and changed the environment."

In the controlled environment of home, mood is within arm's reach. Subtle down-lighting is particularly effective in lacing silver, crystal and china with drifts of light and color. Ideally, the table is lighted from several directions for a natural look.

Candles on table and ceramic window ledge establish the mood, left; frosted strip theatrical lighting above supplements it, reflecting on the ceiling in a blur. Untrapped by the indoors, the night's skyline lights supply a reverse negative view, like an original canvas hung just outside the window.

A wall-hung frosted lantern with 25-watt bulbs low-lights deck dining, right. Inside lights are dimmed for minimum illumination, maximum romantic effect. Candle lighting in protective hurricane chimneys flickers and casts dancing reflections on glass-top table and party chairs.

CHAPTER EIGHT

MULTI-PURPOSE ROOMS

Few self-respecting rooms serve only one purpose anymore. Even a bathroom can be part dressing room and makeup center. A trestle table and benches in a kitchen can be used as a hobby center between meals. A playroom with bunks is also a children's bedroom.

A family room furnished with a sofa bed can easily be converted into a guest room, literally overnight. Books, music, art and good lighting can fulfill a dining room's quieter and more contemplative hours. Many a bedroom includes a place to read or sew.

And, in an open and fluid living room plan, space can serve numerous moods and moments for every family member. What you get out of a room depends solely on what you put into it.

GUIDELINES TO MULTI-PURPOSE ROOMS: CLEVER AND FLEXIBLE

Shrinking space and vanishing maids can be credited with the evolution of an ingenious American lifestyle: The multi-purpose room. Because of changing social and economic patterns, entire specialized rooms have vanished into the past, a nostalgic blur of parlors, salons, music rooms, conservatories and the like. In their places are such jazzy januses as the bed/sitting room, the study/guest room, the living/dining room and the kitchen/family room. All these changes are for the better. Rooms are now evaluated in terms of their self-service, space-saving multiple uses.

It is important to first outline what is required of a room, whether it is your only room or one of 10. Think in terms of sleeping, dressing, living, cooking, dining, loafing and lounging, socializing and entertaining, pursuing hobbies, studying. Think also in terms of the need for privacy and the need for sharing, of places to store things and ways to display things. Now compare these needs with the room's existing space. Visualize how that space might double or triple to best serve your requirements.

The extra-large room is the logical choice for multiple functions. However the super-small room is the one that demands the most ingenuity; yet it, too, can fill heroic roles. Furniture selection, as well as its arrangement, is the key to all useful space. For example, a living room, bedroom or kitchen can easily incorporate dining—a part-time activity. It's simply a matter of choosing a table of multi-use or space-saving design, such as a drop leaf that folds to a slim shadow off-duty. The chairs are equally as well suited to conversational groupings as they are to dining and table games. Some even come on casters to facilitate moves.

A sofa bed, with its living room manners by day, sleeping comfort by night, can help turn even the tiniest room into a guest room part-time.

A one-room beach house, left, illustrates multi-purpose ingenuity with its bed that doubles for sitting, a round table that serves both dining and desk needs, lightweight armchairs for dining or conversation, a buffet that stores clothes plus bed and table linens. Walls are carefree plywood paneled and painted in blue and green stripes.

A family room adjacent to a kitchen, opposite, top, doubles for casual dining. Table and chairs are junk shop finds, restored to social status with fresh paint. Chairs can easily be clustered around the sofa for conversation.

A round table turns living space into a dining place, opposite, bottom. Shelves, wall-hung on brackets, add a third, library/den dimension. Games are played here, hobbies cheerfully pursued.

DESIGN: SHIRLEY REGENDAHL.

DESIGN: SAM PUDER, AIA. SOURCE: JUNE EDWARDS. PHOTOGRAPHY: VINCENT LISAN

A good self-service, multi-purpose room, left, brings the entire family into the kitchen. The large room is systematically divided into three distinct areas: Cooking, dining and conversation. The plan is open and flexible to suit all members of the family.

Storage is consigned to a fanciful, wrought-iron baker's rack. A kneehole desk in the kitchen area serves as a home planning center. The snack bar—improvised with shelf and brackets—seats four on second-hand coffee shop stools, recovered in new vinyl.

A home designed on the open-plan principle, above right, leads from a patio through to a family room, divided from the adjacent kitchen by a snack bar that doubles as a serving station.

Modern materials—vinyl upholstery, laminated plastic counter and tabletops, vinyl flooring—stand up to wear and tear without much care. The room serves numerous purposes—from lounging to snacking to indoor-outdoor entertaining—for both children and adults.

The strategic location of the kitchen, below right, visually separates it from the conversation area beyond without sacrificing the convenience of its proximity. The resulting areas serve both dining and family room functions. The kitchen has a shingled cove ceiling. Wall-to-wall carpet unifies dining and family room areas.

ARCHITECT: JOHN EVANS. AIA. DESIGN: PATTY DOYLE.
SOURCE: JUNE EDWARDS. PHOTOGRAPHY: VINCENT LISANTI.

DESIGN: H. MILLER & SON. SOURCE: JUNE EDWARDS. PHOTOGRAPHY: VINCENT LISANTI.

GUEST/SITTING/DINING ROOMS ... ALL IN ONE

Guest bedrooms have changed so much in the past decade that sometimes the only way they can be recognized is by the bed, and often that is disguised. Sleeping is secondary to dining, TV viewing, conversing, even entertaining, plus a multitude of other activities between guests' visits. Even the sparest spaces are assigned multiple roles.

Unconventional furnishings are responsible for part of the emancipation of the guest room. Beds, often built-in or placed parallel to a wall, are treated more like sofas. Many feature storage drawers beneath and/or built-in shelves around, in place of the usual nightstands, chests and bed of the bedroom "suit." Fabrics assume a living room look. Tables and chairs can be introduced for dining, work or games.

In minimum space, right, a bed has been built in, French fashion, enclosed with draperies rather than the usual paneling. When the tiny alcove is used for dining, the draperies are dropped to discreetly wall off the bed. The drop-leaf table against the wall opens up to comfortably seat six on chairs brought in from other rooms.

In the small open-plan home (opposite, top), cooking, dining, sleeping and living spaces coexist harmoniously. Built-ins form an alcove for the head of the bed. Bedspread and closet curtains are tailored in a non-bedroomy checked fabric.

The beach-house guest room, opposite, below, serves for sleeping, sitting, even dining on occasion. Budget-built, the bed is a latex foam rubber mattress on a plywood platform. Bedspread, bolsters and matching curtains are ribbed cotton ready-mades—all washable. The low Parsons table was constructed of plywood and covered in a vinyl-coated wall-paper; its matching fabric is used here for dust ruffle and curtains. The shag carpeting is easy-to-install carpet squares backed with latex foam rubber.

To save money, and at the same time increase the architectural interest of the room, the structural wall studs were purposely left exposed. Shelves, inserted between studs, hold radio, clock, books and other guest essentials within convenient reach. An inexpensive wicker basket stores linens and towels.

PHOTOGRAPHY: EVERETTE SHORT.

GN: LIZI FREEMAN. PHOTOGRAPHY: EVERETTE SHORT.

GN: LOIS MONROE HOYT, AID. PHOTOGRAPHY: EVERETTE SHORT.

DESIGN: DONALD H. OPPER, AID.

DESIGN: M. GAIL MORGAN, NSID. PHOTOGRAPHY: MALCOLM CO

THE SLEEP-IN DEN AND OTHER RETREATS

Sleep sofas and built-in bunks have helped space to serve smartly without looking utilitarian. And synthetic materials have added years to the life of a room's furnishings.

The quiet retreat, opposite, top, doubles as a guesting place with its sofa that opens up to a queen-size bed. Space around the sleeper-sofa is kept open. Lightweight accent table and ottoman-on-wheels can be quickly and easily moved out of the way. Covering the floor is inexpensive grass matting.

Sectional sofas, opposite, bottom, supply maximum seating in limited space with an option for frequent rearrangement. Wooden block wine racks double as end tables, their pigeon holes filled with magazines. Shelves built into a pecky cyprus wall are equipped with shades that pull down to conceal clutter. A glass-top table, with springy, vinyl-cushioned chrome chairs, fulfills gaming and dining functions.

A garage has been converted into extra living/sleeping/study space, below, for the enjoyment of family or guests. Durable nylon carpet in brown-beige-black-yellow plaid sets the character of the room. Built-in bunks backed with bolsters double for seating. Prefinished plywood paneling covers the walls—all adding up to a nearly maintenance-free, multi-useful room.

DESIGN: VIRGINIA FRANKEL.

DESIGN: EDMUND MOTYKA. PHOTOGRAPHY: ERNEST SILVA.

Hobbies and favorite things theme these three rooms.

The room opposite, fashioned by an eclectic collector, was purposely designed to show off his favorite possessions—the wall-hung Chinese silk rug, clusters of Indian cotton and silk pillows, and brass accessories that range from cricket boxes to tray-top table.

Cushioned sheet vinyl in a harmonizing mosaic pattern covers not only the floor, but storage platform, window seat and couch bases. The dual-duty furnishings in this room are the vinyl-covered couches that double as guest beds.

The maid's room of yesteryear —today's spare—is an ideal place to pursue a hobby. The room above, left, invites creativity. It's furnished with a tabletop surface for sewing, a chest of drawers for stashing fabric, patterns, and thread.

A love seat, upholstered in the same fabric that covers the ceiling, provides a comfortable place to do hand needlework or merely converse with a friend. A good desk lamp provides proper lighting for both areas.

Carpet, closely color coordinated to the carpet on the floor, covers one wall behind the love seat— helping to preserve quiet there.

A family's vacation retreat is well-planned when it serves their multiple needs efficiently, conveniently and attractively. The combination kitchen/ snack bar/living room, above right, does just that.

The snack bar, with a storage unit on each end, physically separates kitchen from living room, without interrupting the flow of conversation between. The handy counter is used throughout the day—for snacking, letter writing, drawing, game playing. Storage shelves— some open, some behind doors— store radio and record player, hobby and other vacation paraphernalia.

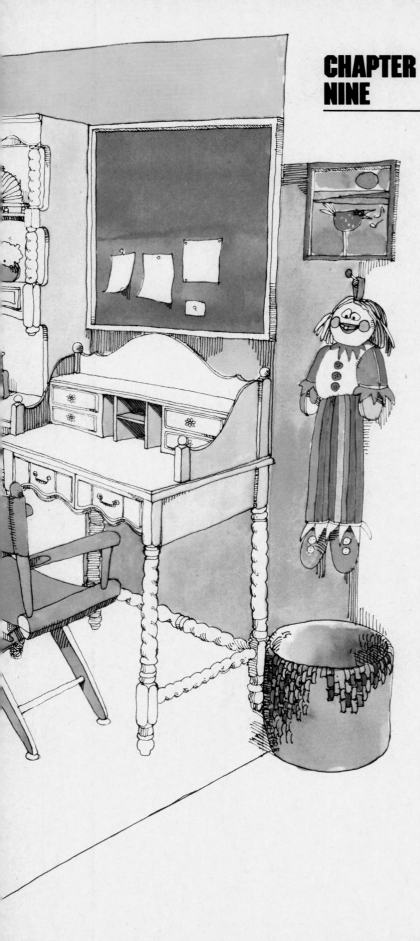

CHAPTER NINE

ROOMS TO GROW IN: TOTS TO TEENS

Today's furnishings are well trained to grow up with children. Chests can start single, low and shallow for Baby's clothes, then stack up slowly to college wardrobe capacity. Finishes are smooth and punishable; corners, thoughtfully blunted.

High-rising, see-through shelves can clearly and fairly divide up space between two children, at the same time storing twin complements of toys, mementos and collections. Childhood is celebrated with bubble gum colors and balloon-shaped toys that gradually concede to the more significant accessories of teen age.

If a growing space is well planned, the most conspicuous change will be the exchange of cradle or crib for bunk or twin bed.

GUIDELINES: ROOMS THAT "GROW"
... HAPPY AND VERSATILE

Color, comfort and flexibility are three keys to furnishing young rooms. Cheerful colors are a "must," especially for tot years. More than pales, primary colors stimulate seeing, responding and learning. As youngsters begin to mature, involve them in the color selections for their own rooms. It will give them a sense of responsibility and individuality.

Comfort is important, not only for the young child but for his parents, too. Space permitting, mother, at least, should have a rocker or chair of her own choosing in the baby's room, since she'll be spending many hours there during his early years. She'll also need a place of comfortable height on which to change and dress him.

Tot-age through pre-teen, furniture should be purchased with consideration for the rambunctious lifestyle. Look for rounded corners, as opposed to shin-bruising, angular ones. Choose storage pieces that will stack to grow with the child's needs. Keep lower drawers free for his personal things with the implicit understanding that what he takes out, he also puts back. Older children delight in chests or storage pieces that have secret drawers or cubby holes for treasures and mementos, and this space should be inviolable if only to show him your respect.

Textures of everything from bedspreads to rugs to curtains and chair seats should be pleasing to

touch, patterns intriguing. Accessories, including toys, are best when they have motion and/or reflection, such as shiny mobiles—again, to invite and encourage response.

Shop with foresight and future years in mind. Insist on well-engineered designs and reputable brand names. Anticipate longevity by investing in chests, dressers and desks gradually, as need dictates. Consider bunching or stacking units that can be added to—a piece at a time, year after year. When cradle is traded for bunk, trundle or twin, the rest of the room should require little change.

A growing room, below, begins with a few basic pieces of furni-

ture, comfortable for mother's use today, convertible to daughter's room with mere removal of the cradle. Patterns are a cheery mix; flooring, vinyl tile, to withstand years of play.

A sleepy, sparsely furnished nursery, right, is awakened by a bold supergraphic rainbow, painted wall-to-wall over the crib by a new father as a surprise for his wife upon her return from the hospital. The room almost glows when the sun shines in, yet can be darkened for slumber, thanks to room-darkening window shades. A chest that's baby-changing height, plus a rocker, are the only other furnishings needed at this time—a nice budget way to start the little one off right.

The ingeniously designed nursery, far right, is less costly than it looks. Colorful, printed, no-iron sheets were used to fashion crib cover and canopy, table skirt and shutter curtains. Storage units are campaign chests with durable plastic tops, used now to hold baby clothes and layette, terry-padded on top to double for a dressing place. Virtually ageless in design, these chests will serve toddler to teen to guest long after the child leaves home. The chrome "bentwood" rocker might be considered a splurge, except it is a long-term investment that will fit handsomely into a living room or master bedroom after the baby is grown.

DESIGN: BRUCE MEYERS.
PHOTOGRAPHY: LAURIE GOTTLIEB.

DESIGN: DAVE FARRAR. PHOTOGRAPHY: VINCENT LISANTI. LOCATION: SOUTH COMMONS, CHICAGO.

GRAPHICS, PRIMARIES, KIDDY SPECTACULARS

A young room, left, designed by two young women, shows what modern mindfulness can do to excite a small, 8′ x 8′ space. No square inch was spared color, texture or provocative shape.

The three primaries—red, yellow and blue—were the starting point; green was used in small, accessory amounts. One wall was turned into a dimensional graphic with numerals cut out of Styrofoam in varying thicknesses and glued on.

Furniture was chosen for its small scale, durable plastic composition and safely rounded corners. The bedspread fabric continues on up the wall adding height to the room. Square and cylindrical end tables double

for storage and adapt easily to the growing years.

Home for two boys, one a fledgling horticulturist, below left, is as decorative as it is durable, as meaningful as it is masculine. Consulted on their favorite colors, respected for their growing interests, the boys are treated to bunk beds covered in predominantly orange, print spreads. Storage campaign chests, all in a row, are color-keyed to each boy's preference and collections.

The plant lover has his own terrariums and his own framed botanical art—easy to simulate by tracing around actual leaves, filling in with color, then framing. The hobby table, well-lighted by small photoflood

reflectors clamped to a shelf, serves for both games and study, one boy to a side.

One small bedroom furnished for girls, below right, includes a self-stick arrow supergraphic that turns an ordinary window shade into an optical illusion. Stripes, colored to match the arrow, are painted down one wall and continued over a corner table constructed of plywood, under which one of the twin beds is stored. Bolsters and inexpensive ready-made spreads turn beds into couches by day.

The mirror over one bed was a door from an old wardrobe, painted and hung horizontally. The rocker, from a junk shop, was painted and recovered.

DESIGN: DAN JUDWICK AND WILLIAM FISCHER. PHOTOGRAPHY: VINCENT LISANTI.

DESIGN: RUDOLPH SALAZAR, NSID. PHOTOGRAPHY: VINCENT LISANTI.

SNIPS AND SNAILS
AND PUPPY DOG TAILS

Consider the plight of growing boys. Until fairly recently they were forced not only to wear blue, but to live with it from birth through teens. And, they were condemned to rooms built like a rancho grande or ship's hold with a minimum of furniture.

In recent years designers and makers have changed all that, among other things, proving it's quite possible for a boy to be boyish living with decent furniture and even non-blue colors, yet grow into a man. Furniture itself has improved to include good-looking, colorful pieces with exciting surface interest, ample storage and hard-knocks finishes—strong enough to survive formative and teen years.

Handsome fabrics are available in everything from masculine linens and burlaps to tweeds and patterns that include un-sissy plaids and stripes—all washable and soil resistant with protection either applied or intrinsic to the synthetic fiber. Today maintenance of a boy's room is incidental; boys can be boys without its destructing.

The boy's room, below, has a washable red-orange-green-blue plaid spread, red-and-white lacquered stacking storage units and a textured rya area rug that literally fills the small floor space, looking like wall-to-wall carpet. On the wall, a novelty rya rug stands in for a headboard.

Boys' bunk room, opposite, top, has neat, uncluttered modern dormitory look. A family with four boys who share one bedroom, solved the problem with built-ins. Mattresses are made up in washable, green-and-yellow plaid and tossed with nests of decorative pillows. Curtains are made to match. Storage shelves and long desk are also built in—around and under the window. The bunks, built for the pre-teen years, remain serviceable through college—ready for whomever is home, plus a roommate or two.

A growing boy is at home both physically and mentally in a room (opposite, bottom) designed with his hobbies, interests, needs and favorite colors. This room has built-in comfort, as well as recreational, study and hobby facilities.

Pre-finished, shale-white paneling, installed horizontally, lines the sleep wall; wood textured hardboard paneling, the others—both highly resistant to scuffs and knocks. The work/study/play area features white cupboards with a desk surface that folds down when not in use. Shelving holds hobby things, portable electronics and excellent adjustable lamp. Masculine stripes in American flag colors dominate spread, shade and floor cushions. Chairs are molded plastic and practically indestructible.

OGRAPHY: KENT OPPENHEIMER.

SUGAR AND SPICE
AND EVERYTHING NICE

Little girls with doting parents are still being brought up in sweet, icing-pink rooms not out of habit but because, according to color experts, pink is a favorite color of little girls. If consulted, they would pick it.

Pink is suggestive of a gentle and affectionate nature. Furthermore, parents often choose pink for little girls because, to them, it reflects a sheltered and indulged existence, most desirable for the female little people.

In the shared pink paradise, below, two sisters benefit by a sophisticated use of mosaic-patterned sheet vinyl flooring—durable, easy-cleanable and when the mood strikes, also danceable. The flooring is continued up a space-dividing

DESIGN: VIRGINIA FRANKEL. PHOTOGRAPHY: HANS VAN NES.

wall and is used to surface a section of the built-in drawers. A vanity/desk on either side of the divide services each girl's dual and changing needs. Hooks hold hats and bags, collected and cherished "things." Each girl's individuality is reflected in her own accessories.

A young girl's dream of a delectably pretty bedroom is realized, at right, in a combination of bonbon pink and green confection colors. Part of that dream is always a "Camelot" canopy bed, preferably full of ruffles.

Both windows and bed are hung with shirred gingham curtains. The bedspread, curtains and pillow shams of the same fabric are all machine washable/dryable polyester and come ready-made. Gingham fabric, available by the yard, also covers the wall. It is shirred onto curtain rods and stretched from floor to ceiling in window-treatment fashion that makes for easy removal for laundering.

A less conventional color choice, below, for youngsters through collegians, is yellow with red-and-yellow print fabric on window shades and ceiling.

DESIGN: ARTHUR LEAMAN, AID.

THE TENDER TEENS: IMPRESSIONABLE AND INDIVIDUAL

A bit of sophistication begins to show in the teenager's room, below. Mother and daughter collaborated on the colors (daffodil yellow and white), as well as on choice of furniture style—American Traditional.

The actual pieces were selected by the parents with consideration for scale in relation to the small room, and for the amount of storage that could be supplied by as few pieces as possible with room left over for daughter's grown-up, panel-style bed and upholstered, ladder-back chair.

The final result includes compact and lightly scaled pieces that make the most of chopped-up wall space, yet yield commodious storage. The furniture is of solid maple in a warm nutmeg finish. And all pieces have matching, impervious plastic tops.

The room, below right, began with a swatch of red-and-white cotton print that prompted an Early American scheme revolving around a Shaker-type four-poster bed. The bed and airy floral spread prompted purchase of a delicately-scaled ladder-back side chair to go with a small, but sturdy, hand-me-down desk.

The combination still lacked sass until it occurred to use the same floral pattern on the walls. The printed swatch went back to work again, matched to its companion vinyl wallcovering that tailored easily to the room's odd juts and recessed window.

The print's red was picked up in a bed throw and curtains. Blue was added in lamp shade, bed pillow, table cover and spread's ribbon trim. Finally, the leftover fabric that started it all was made into a cushion for the little lean ladder-back chair.

A lucky young girl grew up into the charming Colonial bedroom at right. The room, planned long before she was born, was collected through patient but rewarding auction hunts and searches of second-hand shops. Its ingredients are cherished antiques plus authentic-looking, but modern-day, ready-made curtains and bedspread, and medallion-printed wallcovering.

Before the young girl matured enough to enjoy and respect the room, it served as a guest room. After she goes to college, or marries, it will resume its original role. Right now, the thoughtfulness of the room and its treasures, such as the rush-seat ladder-back chair, brass bed, handcrafted wood chests and homemade quilted throw, all serve to increase a young girl's understanding of the past and respect for a tasteful lifestyle.

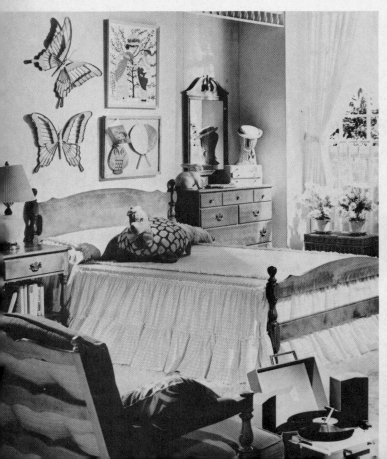 

ROOMS TO PLAY IN: FUN TO LIVE IN

More imagination than money was lavished on the rooms here combining living and playing with sleeping in some cases. In the process of planning such activity environments, it is also possible to bring out the best in youngsters, training them to be responsible for their own rooms by making the rooms not only fun to live in, but convenient to keep in order. Low-cost materials such as vinyls and plywood, assembled in highly imaginative ways, can create a kiddy wonderland that's intriguing, safe, carefree and comfortable.

Boys have their own look-alike, but definitely separate, spaces in the room, above left. Double bunks for each boy accommodate him and a friend. Painted plywood shelters, with ladders up to "2001" tree houses, give each boy a sense of privacy and security.

The room is floored in cushioned vinyl. Toe-soft kelly green carpeting was custom cut to create the grassy private plots that mark each boy's own personal boundaries. The ceiling, covered in acoustical tile, helps baffle sound and preserve quiet for the rest of the family.

The more conventional bed/playroom, below left, can be almost as much fun, especially for the younger set. A network of open shelves, built-in around a window, hold a menagerie of stuffed animals plus infinite amounts of games and toys.

These are the accessories of childhood.

Mini-slat window blinds in alternating yellow and white form a stimulating graphic for young eyes. Flooring is a tweedy shag that helps muffle the sounds of gleeful play.

The super-orderly room, below, was designed by a father for his "tribe" of six, all ages ranging from five to 17. In a home with only one family room for their mutual enjoyment and many eccentric interests, an unspoken tidiness rule was laid down. Each child was assigned his own shelf space and cabinet to show and store things in.

Walls were first covered in black and white plaid vinyl, after which built-ins—constructed of plywood, plus standard kitchen cabinet doors—were added. A ladder permits fun and easy access to top shelves.

This room is used for studying, pursuing hobbies and for entertaining. Kids sleep dormitory-style on an upper floor.

DESIGN: DERRELL BENEFIELD. PHOTOGRAPHY: EVERETTE SHORT.

DESIGN: LORRIE LIEBER AND HADASSAH KINZER, NSID.

CHAPTER TEN

PERSONALIZED ACCESSORIES

From coy nuances to serious collections, accessories are what personalize a home. They tell of wisdom and folly, of search and discovery, of cult and culture.

They prompt conversation and arouse curiosity. Like a bunch of dried weeds, they don't have to be useful. But, like the pottery holding the weeds, they can be. The most humble-born, such as a braided rug, increase in dignity with the years. The most enduring are often impulse items—bought for shape, for color or in a moment of madness, and cherished above all the rest.

Accessories can be serious, whimsical, significant or absurd. It's your unique choice that makes your home distinctively yours.

GUIDELINES TO ACCESSORIES: FREEDOM TO MIX

In today's uninhibited mix of accessories, functional rubs shoulders with fanciful, old with new, traditional with modern, refined with crude. We've gone far beyond the conventional flower painting and mantel clock. Important today is a general enjoyment of accessories, adding color, glamour, humor and character to homes in a free mix of things inherited, discovered, sought out, handcrafted, and even useful items like pots and pans.

Dark wood paneling, below left, shows off a decorative storage corner of copper and brass utensils, plus spice rack, all within easy reach.

A table, below right, shows off the innate relationship of beautiful things without regard to era or origin. Porcelain decoy ducks, leopards and owls are mixed with sterling candlesticks and fine crystal, all pretty and useful accessories.

A room, opposite, top, is transposed in time from the 20th to the 18th century through collected, cherished antiques, considered not only accessories, but also investments.

Modern and traditional mix, opposite, bottom left, in a wall-hung, chrome-and-glass shelf plus wired reproduction of an old oil lamp. Even the striped fabric on the wall can be considered an accessory as it helps "stage" the little writing area.

Kitchen utensils can sometimes stand in for accessories. Conventional copper pots and pans, opposite, far right, are massed and suspended from wrought-iron ceiling hooks, supplying an artistic arrangement as well as a totally useful one.

A collector of Americana has found new uses for beautiful old things, opposite, bottom right. The coffee table is an old biscuit box, set with an antique shaving mirror and a cornhusk figurine. Cog wheels by the fireplace are displayed like sculpture.

DESIGN: JUDITH GURA.

108

PICK-ME-UPS, HAND-ME-DOWNS: FOUND AND SAVED THINGS

What makes a still life of artistic perfection? Four favorite things in balance, opposite, top: A Victorian bust, a gilt-framed portrait, a kerosene lamp, and daisies in a pot.

Turn-of-the-century "finds," far left, ranging from teapot to Mason jars to molds to an old unframed oil painting, line a kitchen mantel.

Grandfather's portrait, far left, bottom, discovered in an attic, prompted a marvelous little massing of portraits. Directly left is proof that wall compositions don't need a central motif —just balance. This merry melange, silhouetted against brick, includes a found clock, discovered printer's blocks and a saved Christmas card.

A simple grouping of inexpensive kitchen items accessorizes a wall, right. Below: A whimsical arrangement of pottery sculpture picked up at the local potter's. Below, right: Hand-me-down clock and china cups.

DESIGN: VIRGINIA FRANKEL.

DESIGN: PAT PLAXICO, AID. PHOTOGRAPHY: MALCOLM COOK.

DESIGN: PAT PLAXICO, AID. PHOTOGRAPHY: MALCOLM COOK.

FOCAL POINT
WALL ARRANGEMENTS

An artful arrangement of accessories in various sizes and shapes, opposite, literally helps the eye tour, leading it from shape to shape, level to level, pausing now at a painting, next at a small tabletop arrangement, then at a lion or an old straw hat. Staged with showcase finesse, accessories are given a backdrop of "weathered" paneling.

A collector of both art and frames draws attention to them, below left, by grouping them in a way that enables prints to hold their own with oils. Art achieves prominence against a white wall with moldings added for a European gallery effect.

Art, below right, is regarded as an investment to be enjoyed and moved from house to house. Some is rented from a local museum loan service, some has been purchased on an installment buying plan. A mix of modern and traditional, oils and prints, are wall-hung by chains from the ceiling to prevent marring the wall and permit changing the arrangement.

Focal point art walls should be interesting enough to make an immediate impression. This can be achieved with innate charm and character or with the element of surprise, like the art on the kitchen soffit, bottom.

DESIGN: ALLISON-REMICK. PHOTOGRAPHY: TAYLOR LEWIS.

SMART WAYS TO SHOW OFF PRIZE POSSESSIONS

DESIGN: DONALD H. OPPER, AID.

The room, left, is planned around a cherished eclectic collection including mirror-faceted pillows, Indian brasses, ceramic leopard, rock collection and fragile figurines.

An entryway, below left, is a gallery for a grouping of prints on the wall plus treasured items: Grandfather clock, Oriental runner and antique cane rack beside door.

A single carved cupid on a wall-hung pedestal, below, is focal point in a vestibule.

A grouping of art and "found" objects decorates the sofa wall, opposite, top left. Simple bandana pillows, opposite, top right, are worthy of space on wicker love seats because of their pattern and color.

One clever designer displays his prized possessions, opposite bottom, left: The wallhanging—from an Indian tent; on the studio beds—Indian pillows.

Pre-Columbian art is played against a modern setting in lighted niches, opposite, bottom right.

DESIGN: WHITNEY CHASE. PHOTOGRAPHY: HAROLD DAVIS.

114

DESIGN: MERLE SHERIDAN. PHOTOGRAPHY: LAURIE GOTTLIEB.

DESIGN: MICHAEL A. TESSLER.

DESIGN: MILO BAUGHMAN.

CHAPTER ELEVEN

OUTDOOR LIVING

Look around you. The sparest patch of grass can become an Eden, the barest terrace, a Babylon. People who are truly outdoor oriented are never stopped at a threshold. Beyond is their milieu, where they can hang plants and light lights; where they can literally plant the brick or sod with springy, supremely comfortable summer furniture, or lash a hammock from post to post or tree to tree, creating a relaxing place in fresh rather than conditioned air, under sun by day, stars by night.

Even the city-bred can enjoy an outdoor environment, whether it means decorating with plantings and treillage inside, or transporting lightweight plastic tables, chairs and chaises, unbreakable dinnerware and battery-operated music to the beach, a park or vacation house.

GUIDELINES TO OUTDOOR LIVING: INSIDE AND OUT

The same essential thought and planning goes into designing for outdoor living as for indoor living. Space is a factor, as are traffic, furnishings, accessories, color and lighting. Backyards and balconies, patios and porches—even postage-stamp-size ones—all have design potential.

Decorating should be tailored to use. The barbecue pit—mainstay of backyard suburbia—is ingeniously constructed for all kinds of charcoal cooking. For smaller spaces, there are portable grills —gas and electric, as well as charcoal—and hibachis, the Japanese charcoal braziers. For entertaining in a large outdoor space, there are picnic tables and benches. Folding chairs and individual tray-top snack tables serve in lesser space.

Ventilation and view can be controlled outdoors by a variety of devices ranging from stockade fencing to a splurge of greenery. And, just as with interior decorating, lighting can be planned for atmosphere—accentuating the beauty of trees and plants—as well as for the functional convenience of extending daytime living well into the night.

Even lacking a plot of "outside," you can enjoy the outdoor look within. Such decorative ploys as green and white treillage, white shutters, awning-stripe shades, billows of ferns and a floor of flagstone-patterned vinyl or wood planks painted with deck paint help project a convincing garden scene indoors. Furniture can be the same durable breed of casual you'd choose for outdoors—wrought metal, tubular plastic or steel, plastic-coated rattan, molded fiberglass or lightweight painted aluminum. Fabrics and other materials can be the same water-repellent, low-maintenance ones.

Decorating needn't stop at the edge of your property. Even a rented vacation place can benefit substantially from a few portable furnishings and thoughtfully chosen accessories.

A large front porch, below left, is screened-in to lengthen its season and furnished with old

PHOTOGRAPHY: CONSTANCE GENTRY.

DESIGN: LEE BAILEY, AID.

wicker restored to grace with a coat of white paint. Inexpensive cocoa matting covers the white painted floor.

On the beach-house porch, opposite, near left, shaggy lime carpet adds a grassy texture underfoot. Supergraphic window shades reiterate the brown of the wicker furniture, the khaki of the sun-resistant slipcovers.

A porch look in a pint-size interior space, below, is achieved with stair rail painted white, wood-patterned wallcovering and plants in wrought iron racks.

The glassed-in sun porch, right, was furnished on a budget with colorful gingham sheets used for cushion covers, tablecloth, shades and curtain edging.

PHOTOGRAPHY: KENT OPPENHEIMER.

DESIGN: MERLE SHERIDAN. PHOTOGRAPHY: LAURIE GOTTLIEB.

PHOTOGRAPHY: VINCENT LISANTI. LOCATION: RIO RANCHO, ALBUQUERQUE, NEW MEXICO.

DECKS, TERRACES, BALCONIES: EXTENSIONS OF INDOORS

An apartment terrace on the West Coast, far left, top, is furnished with chairs fashioned of tubular plastic with canvas seats. A practically indestructible butcher block tops the handy serving cart. Wall art, hung beneath the protective overhang of the roof, is washable fabric on an artist's canvas stretcher.

The enclosed ground-level terrace, near left, top, opens off the master bedroom and is carpeted with green artificial turf. Chaise lounge and table are molded of a durable, weatherproof plastic. The area is dramatically night-lighted by down-lights and tree-hung spots.

An originally bleak Manhattan terrace, opposite, bottom, is made inviting with indoor-outdoor carpet the color of grass. The built-in brick ledge serves both as a planter and for seating. Striped vinyl cushioning survives all but the most inclement weather, when it is easily carried indoors.

The narrow balcony, below left, is designed for maximum use. Furnishing its minimal space are a pair of British officer's chairs, a multi-purpose wrought-iron table and one long, lean wood-and-iron bench topped with red, white and blue vinyl cushions. Natural accessories include potted tulips, fresh fruit and apothecary jars full of edibles. Wall-hung sconces provide mood-making candlelight for dusk and after dark.

The topside deck of a hillside home in the Blue Ridge foothills, below right, literally "grows" out of a shingled roof. The old trestle table, benches and woven-rush side chairs carry out the native wood look. The canvas armchairs are brought out from indoors as needed. The deck is a favorite family gathering place for both meals and entertaining.

DESIGN: WILLIAM KIPKA, A.I.D. PHOTOGRAPHY: HAROLD DAVIS.

DESIGN: WENDELL AND JOAN YOUNG. PHOTOGRAPHY: TAYLOR LEWIS.

DESIGN: FRANCES MOORE, AID. PHOTOGRAPHY: HAROLD DA

PHOTOGRAPHY: VINCENT LISANTI.

DESIGN: VIRGINIA REAF, NSID. PHOTOGRAPHY: HAROLD DAVIS.

PHOTOGRAPHY: LAURIE GOTTLIEB.

Woven grass matting, opposite, serves both fashion and function. Chosen as a natural-looking extension to the house, the matting also serves to protect the patio from strong winds and to filter out the hot California sun. The built-in barbecue area shares the chimney with the family room inside. Built-in cabinets to its right hold all gardening supplies. The lightweight tubular steel chairs work well both indoors and out.

The "yard," top, opening off a family room, consists of poured cement blocks, interspersed with planted areas. The entertaining area is served by a small, portable hibachi on a table made of leftover siding. The flamboyant peacock chairs, lighter than they look and comfortable, are borrowed from the family room. Thin-slatted wood fencing supplies privacy without obliterating the open feel.

A California home, above left, features a patio paved with old brick. A step-up dining area not only adds architectural interest, but also helps separate family activities. Privacy walls of wood and cement block, painted to match the house, give the entire area a courtyard effect. The dining furniture is wrought-iron painted orange. The sunning chaises have metal frames with vinyl straps, all impervious to the weather.

The galleria, above right, of an adobe mission-style house in southern California employs slate-looking clay-baked tile underfoot, rustic wood supporting columns and built-in barbecue of old brick. Over-scaled Spanish-style furniture includes a chunky dining table and handsome Spanish barrel chairs.

Create your own little corner of the world any place, above, with lightweight plastic chaise lounges. Neither sea nor sand will corrode them. The vinyl pads hug either chaise or sand comfortably. The chaise unpadded can double as a table. Matching ice bucket and portable Parsons tables are handy companions.

The same tote-along furniture, right, is equally at home on a windswept waterfront deck. And when the vacation's over, it can be brought indoors for leisure living throughout the house.

DESIGN: BARBARA YOUNG. PHOTOGRAPHY: ERNEST SILVA.

BUYER'S GUIDE

This Buyer's Guide is intended to help you locate pictured furnishings you may wish to purchase. Once you know the manufacturer's name, you can call your local stores (look in the "Yellow Pages") and ask who sells that brand. Or, you can write to Family Circle's HOME DECORATING GUIDE, 488 Madison Avenue, New York, New York 10022, for the name of a store near you. Be sure to state manufacturer's name and page on which picture appears.

Once you have the name of a store that carries the particular brand, go there with your copy of this issue in hand. If you don't find the particular item in stock, chances are the store will be happy to order it for you.

Regretfully, it is impossible to list sources for every single item shown in each picture. Many objects are personal "collected" belongings of the persons in whose homes we photographed. They are presented merely as ideas and hopefully will inspire you to take decorative advantage of your own possessions or to scour thrift shops and attics for special "finds" of your own.

COLOR AND YOU

PAGES 4-5—Furniture designed by Milo Baughman for Thayer Coggin.

PAGE 7—Furniture by Broyhill; carpeting by Wunda Weve; wallpaper by W. H. S. Lloyd; coverlet and draperies by Nettle Creek.

PAGE 8—Wicker headboards and nightstands by Walters; carpeting by Bigelow-Sanford; bedding by Sealy; fabric for bedspreads by David & Dash; lamp by Tyndale; alarm clock by Westclox.

PAGE 9—(Left) Window shades ("Regalite") by Joanna Western; trimming by Conso; fabric by Hannett Morrow & Fischer. (Right) Photo courtesy of Tile Council of America.

PAGE 10—Shag carpeting ("Gordon Hills") by Wellco, of Enka's "Super Bulk" BCF nylon, with latex-foam-rubber backing; furniture and accessories by State of Newburgh.

PAGE 11—Cushioned vinyl flooring by GAF.

PAGE 12—(Top) Vinyl wallcovering (Fashion Personalities "Coral Reef") by General Tire.

PAGE 13—Shag carpet, vinyl tile, furniture and drapery fabric from Sears.

PAGE 14—Photo courtesy of the Hardwood Institute.

PAGE 15—(Left) Etàgere, Parsons table, director's chairs, ceramic lemon/orange tree, ceramic planters and tableware from Sears. (Right) Love seats by Massoud; upholstery and drapery fabric by LaFrance; carpet by Firth; cocktail tables by Medallion; drapery hardware by Graber; floor lamp/table by DeSoto Lighting.

PAGE 16—Furniture by Pennsylvania House.

PAGE 17—(Top) Wallcovering (Fashion Personalities "Homespun") by General Tire. (Bottom) Furniture by Globe, division of Burlington Industries; lamp by Stiffel.

PAGES 18-19—SleepOver sofa, yellow vinyl chair, armchair, ottoman, chrome-and-glass tables and wall shelves, floor cushions, dining table and chairs by Selig; armoire by Vanleigh; white plastic Parsons tables from Lucidity; carpeting ("Artic Circle") by Monarch of Enkaloft spun nylon; vinyl wallcovering (Fashion Originals "Scandia" and "Denim") by General Tire; fabric on walls and window shades by Waverly; laminated window shades by Window Shade Manufacturers Association; chrome table lamp by Robert Sonneman; white china lamp by Tyndale; yellow floor lamp from B. Laytin; dishes and stainless flatware by Royal Copenhagen; painting by Karl Mann; stereo by Sony; other accessories from Azuma; plants from Ethel Rogers.

DECORATING STYLES

PAGES 20-21—Furniture by Stanley.

PAGE 22—Carpet ("Grand Alliance") by West Point Pepperell of DuPont nylon.

PAGE 23—(Top) Furniture by Ethan Allen. (Center) Vinyl wallcovering ("Melinda") from Wall Fabrics Collection by Birge. (Bottom) Furniture ("Sugar Hill Pine") by Plymwood; rug by Bigelow-Sanford; fabric by Waverly; window shades ("Lam-Eze") by Joanna Western; chandelier by Georgian Lighting.

PAGE 24—(Top) Recliner by Berkline. (Bottom) Furniture by Pennsylvania House.

PAGE 25—Furniture ("Westover") by Thomasville.

PAGE 26—Carpeting by Armstrong; furniture by Founders.

PAGE 27—(Top) Furniture ("Benchcraft") by Drexel. (Bottom) Carpeting ("Mascot") by Cabin Craft of Kodel III polyester; draperies by Thortel of Verel modacrylic; furniture and arc lamp by Inter/Designs Ltd., division of Directional; fireplace accessories by Edwin Jackson.

PAGE 28—Furniture by Henredon.

PAGE 29—Furniture ("Kensington") by Drexel.

FLOORS, WALLS AND CEILINGS

PAGE 32—Plywood paneling ("Cedar Weatheredbord") by Evans Products.

PAGE 33—(Left) Photo courtesy of National Oak Flooring Manufacturers Association. (Top right) Plywood paneling (Royalcote "Yorktown Blue") by Masonite; fabrics (for dado, ceiling and tablecloth) by Stroheim and Romann. (Bottom right) Plaid fabric for window shades and tablecloth (of Celanese Fortrel polyester/cotton), sheer fabric in curtains, and fabric ("Plant Life") in picture frames, all by Bloomcraft; laminated window shades by Joanna Western.

PAGE 34—(Left) Vinyl wallcovering ("Bonjour" and "Bonjour Stripe") by J. Josephson; modular seating ("Fibreform") by Berkline; desk chair by Thayer Coggin; globe light bulbs (on wall) by Duralite. (Right) Vinyl wallcovering ("Strictly A Wall Flower" and "Wall Flower's Mate") by Birge.

PAGE 35—(Bottom) Vinyl wallcovering ("Poppies" and "Denim") by General Tire; chairs by Pennsylvania House; tea cart by Ethan Allen.

PAGE 36—(Top) Self-adhesive, brick-patterned plastic ("Stonehenge") by Con-Tact; self-adhesive plastic on table of Con-Tact Extra; upholstery vinyl ("Tortoise") on chairs by Comark. (Bottom) Photo courtesy of Hardwood Institute.

PAGE 37—(Left) Self-stick vinyl floor tiles ("Corrida" Instant-Floor) by Goodyear Tire and Rubber; chairs by Knoll; hanging lamp by Moreddi. (Right) Self-adhesive, high density, latex-foam-backed carpet squares by Jonas; sofa and chairs by Talley Lord.

PAGE 38—Fabric for draperies, shade and seat cushion ("A Study of Trees") by Greeff; carpeting by Lees.

PAGE 39—(Left) Carpeting ("Beau Rivage") by Horizon of Enkaloft spun nylon; lacquer furniture by Jack Norman Furniture Ltd. (Top right) Rya area rug by Egetaepper.

PAGE 40—Carpeting, wallpaper, table and chairs, hanging lamp and all accessories from "Unison" by Montgomery Ward.

PAGE 41—(Top) Area rug by Egetaepper. (Bottom) Cushioned vinyl flooring, wallcovering and fabric for curtains and cushions ("Serendipity") from "Fancy Free" Collection by Armstrong; table and chairs ("Allegro") by Thomasville.

PAGE 42—(Bottom left) Wallpaper, bedspread, brass headboard, chest and lamp from "Unison" by Montgomery Ward.

WINDOW TREATMENTS

PAGE 47—(Top right) No-iron sheets ("Waterflowers" and "Chevron") from "Bed Lib" Collection by Spring Mills, of 50% Kodel polyester/50% cotton protected by Scotchgard. (Bottom left) Traverse drapery rod, chain and holdbacks by Kirsch.

PAGE 48—(Top) Carpeting ("In Credible") by Venture of plush pile Encron polyester; seating pieces ("Trend Seaters") by Crawford; upholstery fabric ("Tempo") by Guilford Mills of Enkalure nylon; window fabric by Richloom of Enkalume polyester; dining chairs by Raymor. (Bottom) Laminated window shades and valances by Window Shade Manufacturers Association; shade trim by Conso.

PAGE 49—(Left) Window shade of Tontine Tran-Lam shade cloth by Stauffer Chemical; fabric by Artmark.

PAGE 50—(Top) Window shade ("Peruvian Stripe") by Stauffer Chemical; fabrics by Design Research. (Bottom left) Window shades ("Comfort") by Joanna Western; vinyl floor by Armstrong; furniture by Woodard; wallpaper by Stockwell. (Bottom right) Window shade ("Baku") by Stauffer Chemical; shade trim by Conso.

PAGE 51—Window shades ("Regalite") by Joanna Western; floral chintz by David & Dash; rug by Edward Fields; wallpaper by Stockwell.

PAGE 52—(Top) All furniture by Flair, division of Bernhardt Industries. (Bottom left) Fabric-backed vinyl wallcovering ("The Morning After") from "Match Maker" Collection by Columbus Coated Fabrics.

PAGE 53—(Top) Vertical shade-cloth (Tontine) blinds ("No Hem" installation) by Thru-Vu; campaign cubes by Kemp; sofa slipcovers of zebra print fabric by Bloomcraft; black chair by Selig; rya rug by Unika-Vaev; lamp by George Kovacs. (Bottom) Beaded window treatment by Beadangles, division of The Papercraft Company.

PAGE 54—(Bottom) Clear plastic plant pots by Plexite Industries; brass chains, courtesy of National Association of Chain Manufacturers.

PAGE 55—(Top) Ceramic-tile window sill by American Olean.

FURNITURE ARRANGEMENT
PAGES 56-57—Furniture from Montgomery Ward.

PAGE 58—Furniture ("Chateau Provence") by Thomasville; carpet ("Sublime") by Armstrong.

PAGE 60—Hide-A-Bed sofa ("Cambridge") by Simmons.

PAGE 61—Rug by Egetaepper.

PAGE 62—Upholstered furniture by Kroehler; wicker chairs by Vreeland; game table by Deutsch; folding screens by Danny Ho Fong; carpeting by S. M. Hexter; painting by Karl Mann; desk table by Russ Stonier; accessories by Raymor.

STORAGE IDEAS
PAGE 66—(Top and bottom left) Cabinetry by Wood-Mode.

PAGE 67—(Top left) Cabinetry by Wood-Mode. (Top right) Bath carpet by Burlington House of Encron polyester; wallpaper by Imperial; towels by Fieldcrest. (Bottom left) Portable washer and dryer by Hotpoint. (Bottom right) Trash compactor from Sears; cleaning equipment by Rubbermaid, David Douglas, General Electric and Quickie.

PAGE 68—(Top) All furnishings from Sears. (Bottom left and right) Sewing machine and dress form by Singer; vinyl flooring by Robbins.

PAGE 69—(Top) Furniture by Founders; no-wax flooring (Solarian "Place 'n Press" tiles) by Armstrong. (Bottom left) Modular storage system ("Rondo") by Domani, division of Burris Industries. (Bottom right) Distressed pine cabinetry by Wood-Mode.

PAGE 70—(Top) Rough-sawn paneling by Evans. (Bottom left) Vinyl flooring by GAF. (Bottom right) Rug (not shown) by Stephen Leedom of Verel/Kodel by Eastman.

PAGE 71—(Top) Carpeting ("Arista") by Collins & Aikman of Kodel III polyester; draperies by Boris Kroll of Verel mod-acrylic; tablecloth and chair coverings by Springmaid of Kodel polyester/cotton. (Bottom) Fabric ("Pedigree Stripe") by Galey & Lord of Fortrel polyester/cotton; carpet ("Star Mist") by Collins & Aikman of Celanese nylon; cabinet, foldaway bed by Seco.

LIGHTING: FOR MOOD AND FUNCTION
PAGE 74—Lighting by Robert Sonneman.

PAGE 75—(Bottom left) Lamp by Tyndale; fabric on window shade and walls by Riverdale; laminated window shade by Joanna Western; dinnerware by Mikasa; placemats and napkins by Vera. (Bottom right) Suspended ceiling with translucent lighting panels and vinyl flooring (not shown) by Armstrong.

PAGE 76—(Top left) Wood-grain paneling by Marlite. (Bottom) Wallcovering by James Seaman; towels by Fieldcrest.

PAGE 77—Vinyl flooring by GAF; appliances by General Electric; sink by Elkay; wallcovering by United-Desoto.

PAGE 78—Ceramic tile on window sill by American Olean.

PAGE 79—Game table and chairs ("LifeStyle") by Syroco, division of Dart Industries.

MULTI-PURPOSE ROOMS
PAGES 80-81—Furnishings from Sears.

PAGE 82—Furniture ("Kensington") by Drexel; deck furniture by Meadowcraft; fir paneling ("Roughtex") by U.S. Plywood; fabric ("Plant Life") by Bloomcraft.

PAGE 83—(Top) Carpeting by Lees; sofa and chair by Conover; draperies by Consolidated Textile; wallpaper by Stockwell.

PAGE 87—(Bottom) Latex-foam-backed carpet squares by Ozite; bedspread and curtains by Bates; mattress of latex foam rubber; wallpaper with matching fabric, courtesy of Wallcovering Industry Bureau; fondue pot by West Bend; radio by Motorola; towels by Cannon; basket by Kessler.

PAGE 88—(Top) Sofa, chair and ottoman by Kroehler. (Bottom) Sectional sofa, ottoman and chair by Bassett, upholstered in fabric of Herculon olefin fiber; party table and chairs by Bassett Mirror; carpet ("Coffee Grounds") by Wellco of Herculon olefin; area rug by Concept International; wine racks (used as magazine tables) by Sarried Ltd.; lamp by Koch & Lowy; painting by Lee Reynolds from Vanguard Studios; radio, TV and stereo by RCA.

PAGE 89—Carpeting ("Brigadoon") by Trend Mills; paneling and doors by U.S. Plywood; desk and chair by Beylerian; lighting by Lightolier; clock by Howard Miller; pillows by Nettle Creek and The Pillowry; clock-radio by Panasonic.

PAGE 90—Cushioned sheet vinyl flooring ("Karachi") by GAF.

PAGE 91—(Left) Sewing machine by Singer.

ROOMS TO GROW IN: TOTS TO TEENS

PAGES 92-93—Desk, chest and deck by Lea Industries.

PAGE 94—Bed, chest, desk ("Sugar Loaf Hill") by Kemp; fabric by Seneca of Celanese Fortrel/Avril; ruffled curtains by Karpel of Celanese Fortrel; rug by A. R. McAuley of Celanese Fortrel polyester/nylon.

PAGE 95—(Right) All furnishings from Montgomery Ward.

PAGE 96—Plastic furniture by Beylerian; Styrofoam by Foam Products Company, carpet from Personalized Carpet Service, paint and materials from Asheboro Concrete Products, all in Asheboro, N.C.; accessories from Arts by Alexander, High Point, N.C.

PAGE 97—(Left) Furniture by Schoolfield; bedding by Simmons; carpeting by Bigelow-Sanford; fabric for bedspreads and shades by Imperial Textiles; toys by Child Guidance. (Right) Bedspreads by Comfy; self-adhesive "arrow" supergraphic designed by Raymond Waites for The Collectors Eye; area rug by Lawtex; wall lamp by Tyndale; portable TV by RCA.

PAGE 98—Rya rugs on floor and wall by Egetaepper.

PAGE 99—(Bottom) Wall paneling by Masonite.

PAGE 100—Sheet vinyl flooring (Foamcraft "Sun Valley") by GAF.

PAGE 101—(Top) Ready-made bedspread and curtains ("Gingham") by Cameo Curtains of Fortrel polyester; carpeting ("Star Mist") of Celanese nylon.

PAGE 102—(Left) Furniture by Ethan Allen. (Right) Vinyl wallcovering with matching cotton fabric by J. Josephson.

PAGE 103—Vinyl wallcovering ("Edgehill" from Jean McLain Collection) by Imperial; rug by Schumacher; bedspread by Bates.

PAGE 104—(Top) Cushioned vinyl flooring, ceiling tiles (Chandelier) and rugs (Lancaster) by Armstrong; chairs by Moreddi. (Bottom) Window blinds by Levolor.

PERSONALIZED ACCESSORIES

PAGE 108—(Left) Refrigerator and double wall ovens by Hotpoint. (Right) Porcelain dinnerware, figurines, faïence boxes by Royal Copenhagen; sterling flatware and candelabra by Danish Silversmiths, division of Royal Copenhagen; crystal stemware ("Largo") by Holmegaard; table runner by Schumacher.

PAGE 109—(Bottom left) Wall-hung chrome-and-glass desk and chair by Selig, fabric on wall by Waverly; lamp by Stiffel.

PAGE 110—(Bottom left) Desk and lamp from Montgomery Ward. (Bottom right) Sofa and love seat ("Country Set") by Kroehler, upholstered in Naugahyde ("Aerflow") by Uniroyal.

PAGE 111—(Top) Carpeting ("Mexicana") by Majestic, of Anso nylon by Allied Chemical.

PAGE 112—Wallpaper by Greeff.

PAGE 113—(Left) Oil paintings, reproductions and prints from SyrocoArt Collection by Syroco; desk and chair by Heritage; lamp by Tyndale. (Top right) Furniture by Ethan Allen.

PAGE 114—(Top) Love seats and chair by Kroehler, upholstered in fabric of Herculon olefin; area rug by Regal; lamps by Tyndale. (Bottom right) Ceiling tiles by Armstrong.

PAGE 115—(Bottom right) Furniture designed by Milo Baughman for Thayer Coggin.

OUTDOOR LIVING

PAGE 118—(Right) Carpeting ("Hawaii") by Galaxy of Kodel III polyester; fabric by Springmaid of Kodel polyester/cotton.

PAGE 119—(Right) Furniture ("Malay") by Meadowcraft; sheets ("Gingham Park," designed by Anita Wagenvoord) by Burlington House.

PAGE 120—(Top right) Chaise and table by Vaungarde of Rubicast by Uniroyal. (Bottom) Indoor-outdoor carpeting of Du Pont nylon.

PAGE 123—(Top left) Peacock chairs, table from Mangurians.

PAGE 124—(Top and bottom) Chaises, chairs, tables and ice bucket ("LifeStyle") by Syroco, division of Dart Industries.